CONSCIENCE

Knowing Right from Wrong

CONSCIENCE
Knowing Right from Wrong

HELMER R. MYKLEBUST, MA, EdD, LittD, LLD

Emeritus Professor of Psychology, Neurology and Psychiatry
Northwestern University

and

Diplomate in Clinical Psychology
American Board of Professional Psychology

THE AUGUSTANA COLLEGE PRESS
MONOGRAPH SERIES NO. 7

The Augustana College Press Monograph Series, No. 7

Published in cooperation with
THE CENTER FOR WESTERN STUDIES
Box 727, Augustana College
Sioux Falls, South Dakota 57197

Library of Congress Cataloging-in-Publication Data:
Myklebust, Helmer R.
    Conscience: knowing right from wrong / Helmer R. Myklebust.
        p. cm. — (Augustana College Press monograph series ; no.
    7)
    Includes bibliographical references (p. 164).
    ISBN 0-931170-65-6
    1. Conscience. I. Title. II. Series: Monograph series (Augustana
College Press (Sioux Falls, S.D.)) ; no. 7.
BJ1471.M94 1997
170—dc21   97-28399
                                                         CIP

Cover Photo: Helmer R. Myklebust in the Myklebust Rare Book
Room at Augustana College.

Printed in United States of America

 PINE HILL PRESS, INC.
Freeman, S. Dak. 57029

Table of Contents

Acknowledgments

Many friends and colleagues have been of assistance in preparing this monograph. I am indebted to them all: pastors, prison staff, inmates, senior citizens and college students. It is a pleasure to acknowledge invaluable support from Ronelle Thompson, Director of the Augustana College Library, from Harry Thompson, Curator and Managing Editor of the Center for Western Studies, and from Arthur Huseboe, Executive Director of the Center for Western Studies, Sioux Falls, SD. The encouragement provided by President Ralph Wagoner of Augustana College is gratefully acknowledged.

My wife, Mary, has been involved throughout, making suggestions and editing the drafts. Her assistance has been inspiring.

Helmer R. Myklebust

Introduction

Values are transmitted through the home, church, school, and other agencies. But we can not but be concerned about how effective our approach is in a complex, demanding society. Questions are asked regarding the nature of values and who carries primary responsibility for teaching them. We are in a period of restricting schools about what can be taught and parents are bewildered about their role. Over and over again we hear the questions, Whose responsibility is it? Who is going to do it? Because of this turmoil, moral values are being neglected. Even clergy question how far the church should go in assuming responsibility for teaching fundamental values. In the past it was assumed that this responsibility belonged to parents. But for many reasons we now ask outside agencies to play a major role in instructing children about what is morally right.

These questions and the attitudes that underlie them reveal confusion not only about who should teach values but about which values should be taught. Children sense this confusion and the consequences are anger, aggression, and violence. They feel alienated and to find answers experiment, sometimes successfully, sometimes in ways leading to criminality. Youth need guidance and direction. To allow floundering is naive and involves unacceptable risks.

Moral values and conscience development are essential. To be indifferent is to invite catastrophe. Behind a values orientation is the fundamental question of right and wrong, but this concept is being neglected. Unethical conduct is on the increase. These circumstances led us to study conscience. The more we neglect distinguishing between what is morally right and what is not the more criminal conduct becomes accepted. It is critical that parents and counselors emphasize moral standards for youth and adults alike. What should be the model for this task? There is no more fundamental approach than to teach the importance and meaning of conscience.

We have foregone this responsibility to the detriment of all. A materialistic orientation has led to moral and spiritual decay. The circumstances before us are disturbing. However, they can be rectified by exemplifying moral values and by a creative emphasis on conscience. There is a direct relationship between immorality and conscience. Unfortunately this relationship is overlooked. Conscience is rarely mentioned as a self-control system or as a frame of reference for moral living.

In making our studies we hoped to increase awareness of the significance of conscience as a basis for what it means to be human. Also, to indicate its importance, not only for professional counselors but for parents, pastors, administrators, educators, psychologists, psychiatrists, and social workers. Conscience is crucial to help people attain their potential and to realize the need for a spiritual awakening.

Conscience is a unique aspect of behavior. It may be weak or disturbed, permitting unfortunate choices, or it may be strong, providing a basis for moral conduct. In this volume the meaning of conscience and its role in the life of every human being is analyzed. Life cannot be understood without the concept of conscience disorders and the disastrous consequences of this condition.

To gain better understanding of this vital self-control system we studied development of conscience in eight groups of people including a population of prisoners. There are consequences when conscience does not develop normally. We hope this discussion will be helpful to every individual who wishes to gain a deeper realization of what it means to live morally. An underlying question is how we value others. Are they only sources of self-gratification or are they valued in their own right as persons capable of distinguishing between good and evil, showing concern and a desire to live in a way that contributes to the benefit of all. Only through understanding conscience can we be the person we are capable of becoming.

CHAPTER I

Conscience-Values-Morality

Conscience has taken on new dimensions as we try to gain control of devastating influences in society. In the past the greatest threats to stability came from outside of ourselves. Today our greatest dangers come from within ourselves—greed, anger, prejudice, need for immediate gratification, and confused values, purposes and goals. The study of values and morality no longer is only an academic pursuit, but a matter of our survival.

Society needs a foundation which places integrity at the heart of all relationships, personal and interpersonal. Shared values are critical to culture, civilization, and society. We cannot exist without them. Only through internalized moral values can we have moral communities. Morality shows concern for others—friends, neighbors, and strangers regardless of race, color, or creed. Everyone has a right to realization of their potential, but not at the expense of others.

Programs to better our lives will not come easily. Many view current circumstances without alarm, not realizing values are distorted, colored with prejudice, intolerance, and materialistic greed. They are unaware that integrity is the foundation of stability. Because of the diversity of our society some question whether it is possible to develop a value system that will provide freedom, hope, and justice for all. Perhaps we need to recognize that irresponsible freedom is equally as treacherous as deprivation of liberty. We are confused and muddled regarding our role as citizens. There is little mention of values that have served humanity since the beginning of time.

The role of values, the psychology and philosophy of right and wrong, must be a guide in our way of life. Development of values is up to us because whether or not we are aware of it we are now determining our future. We are confronted with conflicting influences paraded as a solution to all problems. The need is to evalu-

1

ate these influences, develop a value system to serve as an integrating force, and provide a basis for moral choices. As observed by Lewis, "our disease is the acceptance by culture of immediate gratification" (p. 203). Lewis also refers to social Darwinism as the religion of selfishness, of winning and power. There are other references in psychology and psychiatry saying we are victims of the here and now, that as human beings we have no choice. However, we are recognizing that in a free society we have the luxury and obligation to make the choices that determine our future. In the past we took values seriously but as suggested by Manchester, "this country's values have not merely been restyled, they have been inverted. Our watchword was duty, now it is rights. One's definition of morality has come to depend upon who one is" (p. 9).

There is something missing when society is characterized by crime and poor educational achievement. We create the future—good, bad, or indifferent. To think only in terms of the expedient is to be a child, a wanderer without purpose or meaning. Fairlie reminds us "we must act in the belief, which year by year is confirmed by our science, that there is no man and no woman who cannot be educated to the reconstruction of the future of his society, in order to make life more human for himself and his companions" (p. 242). We have become insensitive to violence, exposing children to disrespect for life; violence begets violence. We must be alert to the trend to view life as being less sacred, more expendable. We have lost the respect our forefathers had for life itself. We must be examples for our youth if we expect them to show respect for themselves and for others.

How shall we approach the problem of insensitivity to values, of what is right and what is wrong? We consider this question throughout this volume stressing that we have neglected the development of conscience, a self-control system which functions throughout our lifetime. We have not given this system the attention required to maintain a moral foundation for all relationships, public and private. What conscience means, how it develops, how it serves as an integrative system and gives meaning to existence must be realized. It is not only in families that we find this lack of awareness. More and more we require that education and values be separate. As a result one of the greatest threats before us is an inability to control violence, intolerance, cruelty, and compulsion for material luxuries. The more secular we become the less regard we have for moral values, and perception of right and wrong lessens. It is common to encounter persons whose perception of wrong is so disturbed that when they see someone being victimized (robbed, raped, or assaulted) they do not realize they are seeing evil. One of our concerns is how perception of right and wrong is changing, how we must be prepared to counteract this trend, a result of secularization.

As a beginning we must understand conscience, how it develops, serves as a guide to what is good, what is evil, and recognize that it is unique. It is the system that makes human behavior possible. Conscience, morals, and values are not identical concepts. We cannot comprehend conscience without recognizing its significance in the development of values and its association with a moral outlook in everyday life. It is the avenue through which we evaluate what we believe to be our purpose in life. Conscience distinguishes us as human beings. It is a vigilant system that warns us of the consequences of our behavior, good and bad. We face a crisis. Unless we are willing to revive feelings of moral responsibility, no socio-political regime can be successful. Feelings of self-control, respect, and honesty cannot be imposed. Real change comes from those who are committed to moral standards that must be maintained through education, government, and business, as well as through parishes and parents. If we work together we have the power needed to gain control of the conscienceless conduct prevalent throughout the world.

The Meaning of Conscience

Conscience has been viewed in a negative sense, as a feature detrimental to living a good life. One's conscience might not be normal, an obstacle to mature emotional and spiritual development, but it serves an essential purpose. Our concern should not be how to eliminate it but how to foster its development. It is through such an enlightened approach that we will become more compassionate human beings and bring about a revival of moral concerns. Political, social, and technological achievements can be effective only when accompanied by moral and spiritual growth. Our precarious survival will deteriorate if we become dependent on policies that do not acknowledge the imperativeness of morality. Deutch in a revealing discussion states, "valuing oneself and others as well as respect for the differences between oneself and others, are rooted in the fundamental moral commitment to the principle of universal human dignity" (p. 513). We are all part of the moral community entitled to respect as well as justice. Covey says conscience is "a deep inner awareness of right and wrong, of the principles that govern our behavior, and a sense of the degree to which our thoughts and actions are in harmony with them" (p. 70).

In his book *The Closing of the American Mind,* Bloom argues that we have become a people without connections, with emphasis on openness and relativeness; there is no right or wrong, only the opinion of someone who expresses his views. Without moral standards, without principles and convictions we have no values to generate the cohesiveness essential in a democracy, essential to civilization itself. It is the lack of ideals, the attitude of indifference, the cynical feeling that nothing matters that led to our investigation of what conscience means and how we can counteract the feeling that all is relative; "all I need to do is to prepare myself to out-do others, no matter whether it is right or wrong because moral values are only outmoded concepts anyway." Such reasoning leads to catastrophe. We are seeing it in delinquents and criminals. Raine refers to this problem as deficits in moral reasoning. Poor ability in moral reasoning is related to criminal behavior and is apparent in children even before ten years of age; if not corrected they become criminals as young adults. Moral reasoning is the process through which conscience develops and self-control attained.

We need convictions and beliefs. Simple openness is equivalent to aimlessness. All great music, art, literature, and science has been developed by individuals of purpose, individuals showing commitment, involvement, and aspiration. Values and beliefs were recognized and gave coherence to daily life. These creators found meaning because of their convictions. Education should not consist only of training for a career, but provide a framework for ethical living with emphasis on the significance of moral values. A fundamental change is required based on the concept of moral principles and what we can do when convinced we can achieve the highest levels of our potential.

A look at newspapers, magazines, and television reflects that nothing is held sacred. Judging from the popularity of certain television programs we enjoy watching suffering, with the possibility that day by day more horrendous episodes of human degradation will be available to observe. Why do we condone portrayals of violence and degradation without realizing their impact as models? Because we do not respect the dignity of every human being. We must be aware of aggressive trends in children and help them learn to resolve conflicts without violence, help them learn the meaning of feelings, that name calling, racial slurs, and anger provoke hostility. Such training is primarily the responsibility of parents because the family is the center for moral training.

We have great traditions, achievements, and teachings; a great moral heritage that is being ignored. There is little reference to spiritual and moral values. To teach children and youth only what is useful vocationally is deadening. Right and wrong also must be taught, including beliefs, feelings, convictions, and the meaning of personal integrity. Families must do more than play together. They need to trust their beliefs and reflect the importance of the spiritual, sacred, eternal, and ennobling, if children are to grow up to be morally responsible. This is moral education. It can be accomplished when we believe that what is right and what is wrong matters more than anything else we teach children. Conscience is the paradigm for humanness, for being spiritually aware and in tune with life. Idealism is the basis for desire to improve. Human beings are capable of becoming. The views expressed by Fairlie help clarify the importance of conscience.

> Our societies have systematically undermined our consciences, the place where our selves are rooted and admonish us. There is not one of us who does not feel the bidding of conscience, know that it is a commanding voice in us to be obeyed or disobeyed at risk, and yet find ourselves deafened to it by voices that tell us that we may painlessly disregard it. (p. 206)

Fairlie further states that it is conscience that tells us how to be human and "since societies in effect have surrendered any pretense to virtue they are content that we should abandon any claim to it as well" (p. 210).

One cannot but wonder why we do not talk more about evil when our daily lives are fraught with so much that is damaging. Why do we ignore corruption? We rarely think in terms of good and evil, not realizing it is essential to work toward good and resist the evil around us. We no longer fully recognize what being human involves. If we cease being able to imagine our true humanness it will drop away from us, a tragedy which must be avoided. Dupré warns that a neutral definition of good and evil is not sufficient. The magnitude of evil is great, and without perception of what it means we become deadened. We hear that science and values are opposites, that to be scientific is to be conscience free, that one cannot be scientific and engage in values simultaneously. Fortunately, this rationalization seems to be diminishing. Smith, in an important contribution, states that science and conscience cannot be kept in isolation. Both are a means for seeking truth, the focal point of self-understanding. Science is based on standards of morality without which it cannot be considered a trustworthy endeavor; but it depends on the scientist's understanding that science is based on standards of honesty and integrity. Evil must be resisted at every level, in our personal and professional lives. Perhaps the most difficult aspect of this concept is that evil cannot be overcome with evil. Corruption and criminal violence can be reduced only through adherence to moral values, through demonstration of integrity. Moral values are teachable through example and instruction. We can show others life has purpose and that there is a role for each of us. We can be meaning-makers and assist others in finding their mission.

Meaning

Conscience gives us the ability to serve both as observer and the one being observed. No other quality of mind is more indispensable for attaining meaningfulness. It is the process that keeps our ideals and standards of excellence before us. We have no other means by which to judge the quality of our behavior and the behavior of others. Standards of right and wrong must prevail throughout life. This "self-referential" process provides a model for civilized behavior. We serve as our own witness and compare what we have done or contemplate doing with moral standards that should be maintained. Through conscience we identify ourselves as persons whose constructs of right and wrong are binding. These constructs are not foreign because they have been internalized as part of our being. If our conduct is mandated by external controls, what we do is not a function of conscience. Conduct not determined by conscience can be judged only in terms of legalities, not in terms of the excellence of human achievement. When viewing conscience as the system for self-appraisal we do not conceive of it as an oracle that talks to us in the manner of a policeman's voice, never making mistakes or leaving no alternatives. Rather, it is a system which provides the basis for making decisions. As in all human judgments, however, errors may be made. This underscores the fundamental truth that we must strive to develop the highest level possible of right and wrong. A primary gift of being human is that we can cultivate moral knowledge; no other form of life develops morality. Moral standards are complex, involving the rights and dignity of other human beings. But knowledge alone does not serve as the basis for conscience. Values such as honesty and integrity must be incorporated. Conscience determines the ways in which knowledge is used. Purpose becomes critical. Without consideration of purpose knowledge can be misleading, self-indulgent, or even dangerous. For example, sex education programs have not reduced the number of teenage pregnancies. Knowledge was provided without emphasis on moral values so there was little effect on conduct. The same situation prevails in treatment programs for prisoners. Vocational and other types of rehabilitation programs are provided without reference to the moral values that make living in society possible. The result is that recidivism has not been reduced. While knowledge is critical when gained without reference to moral principles, it does not necessarily cause people to conduct themselves in responsible ways.

Bloom's analysis of the deterioration of values in our society includes the suggestion that what each generation contributes depends on what it adds to the long, endless concerns of human beings. Why do we proclaim that our standards are better than what characterizes much of our era? There are many reasons, one of which is that simple openness, the approach which says teachings of past generations are flawed and irrelevant, obliterates the search for truth and excellence. History does not teach that all is relative. As Bloom states, "yet the fact that there have been different opinions about good and bad in different times and places in no way proves that none is true or superior to others" (p. 39). Openness as an approach to excellence flows with what most immediately contributes to self-indulgence. Virtue is not a way to gain advantage and privilege. As Bloom insists, commitment is a moral virtue and leads to life-enhancing behavior. Simple openness leads to lack of conviction, just as egalitarianism leads to lack of creativity. It is value creation as represented by conscience which determines excellence in our lives and in history as well.

Definition

The term conscience has a variety of meanings as found in theology, philosophy, science, literature, and psychology. A dictionary of psychology defines conscience as the attitude of one individual toward the moral and social implications of his behavior, involving judgment of value; conscience is experienced when one is presented with an incentive to violate an ethical principle previously recognized, characterized by an emotion of shame or remorse. Although this definition includes aspects of conscience, it does not comprise a satisfactory base from which to understand this feature of the human mind. It states conscience is an *attitude*, whereas it is more a process for evaluating and integrating experience. Also, this definition states it functions only when we are confronted with a choice that violates ethical principles. Actually, conscience functions constantly, often serving as the basis of judgment without feelings of shame being present. The definitions found in some dictionaries are more inclusive, saying conscience is:

> a sense of consciousness of moral goodness or blameworthiness of one's conduct, intentions, or character, together with a feeling of obligation to do right or to be good. Hence it is a faculty, power or principle conceived for deciding the moral quality of one's own thoughts or acts and defining what is good. (*Webster's Collegiate Dictionary*, 5th ed, 1986)

Another dictionary definition says that conscience is the:

> internal recognition of what is right and wrong in regards to one's actions and motives; it is the faculty that enjoins one to conformity with moral law; the faculty which decides upon the moral quality of one's actions and motives; the still small voice, inward monitor, moral faculty, moral sense of duty, moral obligation, call of duty, moral consciousness, scruples, and compunction. It provides the basis for integrity. (*Webster's New Collegiate Dictionary*, 1973)

These definitions provide a substantial base for understanding conscience. Instead of being described as an attitude, it is characterized by terms such as a faculty, a sense, a power, an internal monitoring process, a voice, a moral sense, an obligation to fulfill a duty, and the basis for integrity. We have integrity to the extent that we have developed a mature conscience and live up to it. Conscience, indeed, is related to the behavior referred to when we speak of integrity. But as a system of self-appraisal it can function only when properly developed, when individuals have knowledge on which responsible decisions can be made.

It is helpful to consider what is meant by moral or morality and ethics or ethical. These terms are related to the concept of conscience. Morality refers to actions without judgment of conduct. However, when we say conduct is morally faultless we refer to the excellence of behavior. Another way of describing morality is as the outward manifestation of one's conscience, conduct as observed, whereas conscience entails judging conduct itself. It is possible for an individual to behave morally through external, supervisory controls without having developed a mature conscience. Morality is a code of behavior accompanied by feelings of obligation. Ethics is a science concerned with the study of morality including good and evil. It is concerned with principles of morality. As a science the study of ethics investigates the activity of individuals not as events, but as judged by moral standards.

Superego, a term first presented by Freud, is used in psychology and psychiatry to refer to much of what is meant by conscience. Bostrom states, "Freud's view is that conscience, or superego, guides a person as a parent does an infant. An infant needs a parent to restrain and prod him. In the same way, the growing child, the adolescent, and the adult need the restraining and prodding mechanism within themselves" (p. 289). Freud defined the superego as that part of the personality which criticizes the ego and causes distress, anxiety, and feelings of punishment when the ego engages in impulses emanating from primitive, instinctual feelings. In Freud's era the problem of a punishing conscience was prevalent, leading to emotional trauma and suffering. In contrast the major problem before us now is that parents and society as a whole are unusually permissive, providing only moderate, inconsistent standards and an attitude of indifference which implies "anything goes." The result is diminishing moral standards and underdeveloped consciences. We must emphasize integrity if we are to restore moral values as a foundation for emotional health and well-being. The outlook is encouraging because authorities are talking about an "immoral conscience" and a "sick" conscience. When we see persons who fall into these categories we look for problems of physical, emotional, and spiritual health, recognizing that usually the problem is one of unfortunate training in early life because the health of an individual's conscience reflects his moral upbringing. This point of view is urgent because of the connotation that conscience causes suffering and should be eliminated.

We must become aware that to be human is to have a conscience which serves the basic purpose of fostering uprightness, the system that preserves humankind itself. It is the means whereby we become aware of what constitutes good and evil. A neutral attitude, common in a society of relativism, deadens perceptions so we do not care about what happens around us, leading to greater and greater degeneration and alienation. Many attitudes about what constitutes wrong versus right are minimized. We are more relative about honesty assuming shoplifting and tax evasion are a way of life. The most serious shift in attitude is indifference regarding the sacredness of life. Murder, rape, assisted suicide, and gang violence are seen as necessary evils in a highly secularized community. This deadening of perception must be recognized. Conscience is more than a punishing superego.

As emphasized by Ledereq morality provides rules governing conduct. Certain behavior is perceived as praiseworthy and other behavior as blameworthy. Those who act morally are viewed as good, virtuous, and trustworthy leading to homogeneity in society. Moral conduct leads to inner dependence and inner strength, a precious state of being. It is seen as inner vision, an answer to the meaning of life. This inner vision, at least in part, is developed by comparing one type of conduct with another, not only what is flagrantly right or wrong but good conduct with conduct that is very good or very bad. Moral consciousness is linked with a sense of duty, the basis for making wise decisions, the foundation of wisdom, the opposite of naive openness and relativism. When moral behavior is not achieved the mind cannot be at peace. As Ledereq insists, "Good is an absolute and must be done unconditionally" (p. 16). This is not a simple process that can be determined forever.

We are perpetually in need of making choices, but we have the ability to strike a balance, realizing that what is simple often is wrong.

Origin of Conscience

Reference to conscience goes back centuries. According to Dummelow, Adam and Eve did not have a conscience until they disobeyed the command given by God. Prior to this they were in a perfect state in paradise and did not need a conscience. Only after they had disobeyed did they realize there was right and wrong. Where there is no evil there is no need for a conscience. Dummelow explains the experience of Adam and Eve by saying:

> The first result of disobedience is the awakening of conscience. They lost Eden and they gained a conscience. The whole story of the Fall is a parable of every sinner's experience. In every temptation there is an exciting cause without and an answering inclination within; every act of submission to temptation is a choice exercised by the will; and the result of sin is an uneasy conscience and a haunting sense of shame. (p. 9)

Are we born with a conscience? Many people believe that we are. But these individuals may not be differentiating between conscience and soul. Nelson (1978) explains, "the capacity to develop a conscience is innate but the content of conscience will come from society" (p. 28). This point of view is supported by scientific studies of moral development. Capacity to acquire conscience is innate, but it is the responsibility of adults to foster its development in children through example and training. This is one of the most vital aspects of parenthood.

If we view conscience as the voice of God we might think of it as being inborn, perhaps relating to the soul. It is necessary to differentiate between soul and conscience although there is a relationship between these facets of our being because conscience serves as a guide to moral behavior and living a life of virtue. Beliefs concerning the origin of conscience are of interest in other ways. If we believe it is inborn we might assume it is a fixed entity much as we assume the soul is not under our control; it exists without our being directly involved with it. These beliefs cause us to be oblivious to the importance of conscience.

In discussions of conscience we are trying to better understand one of the most intimate, delicate, complex features of what it means to be human. Rehwinkel analyzed this human characteristic and warns that conscience cannot develop and function normally when mental faculties are impaired. We are making progress in understanding that when the mind is not normally developed, as in the profoundly mentally retarded, or has seriously deteriorated, as in persons with Alzheimer's disease, conscience cannot function adequately. In these instances there has been no effect on the soul, but self-control mechanisms either have not developed or have deteriorated, leaving these individuals in need of external controls of the type required by children.

Magid and McKelvey argue that we are raising conscienceless children and suggest that what we have before us is an increasing number of psychopaths. This diagnostic term is used for adults who commit serious criminal acts without feelings of remorse. Because they feel no remorse they are thought to be without a conscience. This is but one aspect of the problem before us. There are other features of immorality including an attitude of indifference and condoning immoral conduct. The main concern is not to get caught. All adults, not only parents, must assume responsibility for the lack of moral values.

Conscience and Obligation

The writing of Chambers some years ago is pertinent. He says conscience is "that faculty in me which attaches itself to the highest that I know, and tells me what the highest I know demands that I do" (p. 134). He believes conscience as a faculty not only points to what is right but carries within it the connotation that it be obeyed. Our responsibility is to keep our conscience sensitive; what a responsibility this is! When conscience becomes dulled the consequences are unimaginable. The task of every human being is to be sensitive to what is morally right and to behave accordingly. We are defeating ourselves when we argue with or bribe our conscience. The only road to spiritual freedom is to accept the role of conscience, to do everything we can to foster its development and insist on moral conduct from ourselves and others.

In further consideration of what conscience means we must recognize that it is made possible through memory. When we provide the basics of right and wrong conduct our children learn through remembering what we have taught them. If conscience were present at birth, as in the case of the soul, training and memory would not be involved. We develop a conscience only when we are given the training and example necessary and when these experiences are stored in memory and serve as a guide for conduct. Chambers cautions against the "shallow insecurity of the present" (p. 134). Indeed, if we do not build a foundation day by day for a moral approach to life we are in constant jeopardy, as is everyone with whom we come in contact. Long provides an interesting conclusion when he says, "all ethical living involves a tension between what men ought to do and what they can do" (p. 15). But what we can do is often overlooked. We must realize that we are not achieving that of which we are capable. To gain this higher level of our capabilities we must teach children about good and evil and provide them with an example of what good conduct means. As Coles so aptly states:

> Whence the voices? They came from mothers and fathers of course—introjects they are called; and by school age are quite solid presences in a child's life, a psychological force whose everyday influence on the young can be ascertained without too much difficulty, if enough time is spent watching and listening. (p. 8)

Allport (1951), a pioneer in the study of conscience, observes, "conscience is the indicator of the measure of agreement between our conduct and our values, whatever they may be" (p. 90). Hence, conscience serves as a mediator and is more than a judgmental process. But the way conscience functions is influenced by the circumstances in which we find ourselves. For example, Milgram (1974) states, "when the individual is working on his own, conscience is brought into play. But when he functions in an organizational mode, directions from the higher-level component are not assessed against the internal standards of moral judgment" (p. 130). His observation is critical in understanding mass movements that are destructive and catastrophic in cruelty, such as the Holocaust. By inference our control system can be overridden because of adherence to external authority. This possibility warrants careful analysis of the ruthless violence, religious or other-

wise, that leads to mass cruelty. Messner, a psychiatrist, has contributed to our understanding of this issue by relating his own
experience after being elected to public office. He found he was
allaying his conscience through rationalizing that it was for the
public good. After some self-evaluation he found he had undergone
an alteration of his conscience. It is apparent that if we relinquish
our inner monitoring process to the demands of others, no matter
how influential these individuals might be, we can become victims
of blind compliance. The extent of this problem in circles of government, business, or cults has not been determined but it is a feature of "public morals" worthy of caution. Conscience must not be
relinquished no matter what the circumstances. Giving up our self-
control system is a dangerous step. It can lead to self-destruction
and to the destruction of entire societies.

A Monitoring System

Hallesby says conscience can be distinguished from instinct
and operates before, during, and after the action involved. As a
monitoring system it renders judgment but also informs us of what
is right and wrong. It expresses itself without providing explanations and does so in absolute, not relative terms. It does not make
the moral rules, but passes judgment on them. It acts without our
asking it to, whether we want it to or not. Often we find its judgment is inopportune, but as our mediator it must alert us to what
we should do. It warns us of our deepest motives. Having a conscience assumes we can tolerate suffering because often our
behavior involves paying a price physically and emotionally.
Maintaining a mature conscience is an ongoing process. As we
grow older it may become less arduous, but it degenerates whenever we shirk moral responsibility. Keeping our conscience active
is required if we are not to deteriorate and become less than fully
human. This is the greatest challenge we face in life but it is worth
the price we pay for not drifting into indifference.

Situational morality prevails when we conduct ourselves on
the basis of what we can get by with. If we are not in danger of
being caught we do whatever is pleasing without concern about
what is morally obligatory. When we conduct ourselves in this way
values become a function of whims, what we choose according to
our pleasure. Integrity is vital, not only for ourselves but for others.

Conscience functions without pondering what ought to be done. It warns and informs us without putting the message into words. It is when we argue with the message, when we want to rationalize or bribe our conscience, that we talk to ourselves.

Some authorities object to the inference that conscience is a control system because it implies that a unitary psychological structure is in control of behavior. A number of attitudes make up our personality, all relevant to how we conduct ourselves. But we need to recognize that feelings and attitudes are monitored through conscience, that this control-system is basic to understanding children and adults. Only through developing a mature conscience can we avoid being controlled by others. If our control system is inadequate we are dependent on others for direction. An inner regulatory system is the basis for independent, responsible behavior. It is the basis for being able to say no to impulses that must be controlled if we are to survive and live independent lives. We refer to those who attain a mature conscience as having acquired the "art of living." They have acquired the basis for "peace of mind." This level of human behavior involves struggle against evil, bearing in mind that conscience is not a fixed entity and that it is always growing and changing without relinquishing its purpose. This change for most people is toward greater maturity, toward love of oughtness, and sacrificial behavior.

There is a need for greater attention to conscience as a monitoring system, as seen by violence in the street, abuse in homes, and abuse in the workplace. Abusiveness has increased, indicative of ways in which the construct of right and wrong is being neglected. With the growth of multicultured circumstances it is increasingly apparent that moral values must be adhered to if every individual is to be shown the dignity to which he is entitled. We cannot adhere only to old patterns. We must develop new ones to meet new circumstances, recognizing that moral values do not change, but the pattern of deterioration in interpersonal relationships does.

Conscience and Corruption

Kolenda makes us aware of the urgency to understand conscience as well as the results of not recognizing its importance saying that:

part of the impetus behind this change—is clearly attributable to the alarming proliferation of dishonest practices in the public arena. When congressmen are sent to jail for bribery, when prominent businessmen are tried for tax evasion, when prestigious investment firms are fined millions of dollars for cheating the public, the concern with ethics is not surprising. (p. IX)

His observations stress that dullness of conscience leads to disintegration at all levels of society. We cannot overstate the fact that a mature conscience is the foundation on which feelings of responsibility rest. Macquarrie makes this point when he states that conscience is a summons to the full humanity of which we are capable. He continues:

It is a call to that full humanity of which we already have some idea or image because of the very fact that we are human at all— although we commonly think of conscience as commanding us to do certain things, the fundamental command of conscience is to be. (p. 158)

The challenge is that we recognize our humanness and work toward its manifestation. It is through conscience that knowledge and feelings converge so that we can be free and responsible citizens. As Lehman says, "conscience is the bond between law and responsibility—-the bond between duty and obligation" (p. 33). Educational agencies are not teaching the importance of values. Churches and synagogues emphasize moral principles, but conscience is rarely mentioned. There is a great need for understanding conscience. Because of its significance in how we conduct ourselves it should be included in curricula at all levels of education: elementary, secondary and college. Departments of philosophy and psychology should provide courses that explore all aspects of self-regulation.

However, some scientists have studied the meaning and significance of conscience. An example is the work of Blasi. From his viewpoint moral action is mainly a question of self-consistency. Moral behavior, he states, involves three central psychological concepts: (1) identification of oneself as a moral person or the self as moral, (2) responsibility, extending oneself into moral action, (3) self-consistency, showing integrity and character (p. 129). This analysis helps us realize that insincerity, deceitfulness, and super-ficiality do not lead to moral living. We can live morally only when we choose to be a moral person and take responsibility for living that way. Blasi's analysis raises the question of the relationship between moral knowledge and moral action. Usually we know what is morally right but to act morally is another matter. Self-consistency and integrity are critical. If we have not identified with what is right it is unlikely we will act morally even if we have knowledge of what ought to be done. Moral ideals, although essential, are effective only when we identify with them. According to Blasi:

> Moral judgments reflect the individual's general understanding of himself, other people, social relations, and institutions; this understanding can and does change as a result of the development of one's intelligence and of a richer and more complex experience with the social world. (p. 129)

The extent to which individuals identify with what is right varies because many have not developed a mature conscience. When we identify with what is right moral action is assumed. This is the basis of self-consistency, often defined as integrity.

Living Morally

Taking responsibility for behaving morally is a process, not a fixed state. It entails making choices, big and small. As reported by Nelson-Jones, "responsibility is an inner process in which people work from inside to outside" (p. 37). When we suggest people be morally responsible we do not mean they should always take blame for what occurs, but that they should explore avenues through which they can be effective in representing what is good and refrain from evil, becoming secure in this way of life and assisting others in doing the same. Many never attain this kind of self-validation. They continue to be fearful of doing what is right and perpetuate feelings of distress and inferiority. The study of evil, how it debilitates all aspects of life, has been neglected. Evil must be studied in relation to what is good because without good-ness there can be no evil. Morality and values are not relative. Peck makes this point when he states, "the central defect of evil is not the sin but the refusal to acknowledge it" (p. 69). Another viewpoint is given by Roberts who says "even if scientific visions are rid of false objectivity and based on personal commitment to the truth, a scientifically dominated world can never diminish the appalling disproportion which now exists between intelligence and virtue" (p. 69). His observation epitomizes the theme of this volume. Science and new knowledge are basic to living in a computerized world, but to assume that this alone can form the basis of values needed for a moral society is perilous. We need only be aware of the corruption at many levels to realize that other factors must be brought into play. It is these factors we include under the concept of conscience. We must recognize the importance of honesty, integrity, kindness, dignity, and other moral values if we are to overcome what Roberts describes as the appalling gap which exists between intelligence and virtue.

We live in a society which requires us to fulfill many roles making it easy to become inconsistent, if not disintegrated. We shift into the roles required by organizations in which we are employed or those from which we gain social prestige, including those existing only for political or professional purposes. Often our integrity is put to test. As Taylor suggests it is those of us who keep our inmost self intact, "whose self is whole and integrated" (p. 144), who resist being swayed into doing what is wrong even when the "group", those in power, press us to join immoral activities. Immoral behavior must be seen for what it is if we are to gain control of decadence. Our educational institutions place emphasis on the development of intellectual skills, training physicians, engineers, economists, accountants and business people. The person, the sense of caring, empathy, and integrity are omitted. Sometimes students are viewed as commodities to be prepared, packaged, and delivered; people become things. When moral values are ignored we foster a culture of privilege, reverberating around the objective of how much can I produce for self-indulgent purposes. Kitwood observes, "to trust other persons is, in a sense, risky even under the best of circumstances, since it carries the threat of betrayal, or even of annihilation" (p. 224). He concludes that moral progress will be slow and "encounter enormous psychological difficulties." This may be true but we have given only token attention to the significance of conscience, to values that clarify the nature of what is good and what is not. Psychology, the science of human behavior, at times has depersonalized human beings and not stressed the development of our most human capacities, to idealize, to inspire, and to love. Morality cannot be delivered to another person. It can be taught only through consistent example and guidance. It entails deep respect for the integrity of others, commitment to what is right, and to the principle that development of character is paramount no matter what the circumstances. Only through integrity can we live a consistent moral life. Integrity and consistency go hand in hand and form the basis of responsibility. Our lives always involve organization and inevitably we must have the strength of character to assist in establishing the moral atmosphere that prevails. If an organization violates moral standards we have only one choice, to do what is right and to allow our conscience to function in the most effective manner possible. We can accept only those patterns, rules, and practices which do not violate our standards if we are to retain our identity as a moral person. To do so is of utmost significance, not only to ourselves but to all with whom we come in contact. Antonovsky studied the relationship of health, stress, and coping to moral behavior, finding that coping is strongly related to a "sense of coherence." He states:

> the sense of coherence is a global orientation that expresses the extent of which one has a pervasive, enduring, though dynamic, feeling of confidence that one's internal and external environments are predictable and that there is a high probability that things will work out as well as can reasonably be expected. (p. 123)

Values

Conscience and values are inextricably related. Because of their importance in all phases of moral behavior values need to be emphasized. Kilby in his book, *The Study of Human Values*, provides insights into this aspect of living. His emphasis is that the value orientation of a culture forms an interlocking network of influences from major to minor significance varying from "musts" to "oughts" and "shoulds." Williams (1968) defines values as "criteria or standards of preference" (p. 33). He further states, "values

are conceptions of the desirable or worthwhile" (p. 36). Values
have a profound influence on conduct and, according to Williams,
"give structure to a life and point the way to the future. Beliefs and
values together supply the ground plan of existence for each of us"
(pp. 55-6).

We face turmoil about values and how they should be conveyed. But many adults struggle with what they believe is important, the way in which they want to live their lives. No more basic
question confronts us in our lifetime. As Kilby notes, "the most
common if not also the most important role of values is as standards of judgment" (p. 61). He also says, "moral values are necessary for group functioning" (p. 63). Each of us must voluntarily do
what is right if our group is to carry on daily activities successfully.
Moral values are internalized judgments that make up conscience.
Kilby states, "the capacity for conscience is innately supplied" (p.
66). Values give meaning to existence and each of us has a responsibility in this meaning-making process. Perhaps few of us realize
that our role as meaning-makers is one of the most significant
responsibilities we have as adults, especially as parents. Often we
fail in adequately helping others gain meaning from what is taking
place in their lives. We do not communicate values because we
have not attained the level of meaning necessary to integrate what
is happening in our own lives, despite the fact that values provide
the stability for successful living. Those who have standards and
beliefs about values are better adjusted and more effective in handling the conflicts and setbacks that occur.

Moral values cause us to feel that we will do what is right. They
provide a sense that life is meaningful, consisting of more than the
here and now. Values are the basis of our wanting to be what we
should be. Values provide the standards we need to be "moral rea-
soners." Although rarely mentioned, children benefit from being
taught the seven deadly sins of pride, envy, lust, sloth, gluttony,
covetousness, and wrath. They should be taught the meaning of the
ten commandments. These teachings reflect what we have learned
about values. Marital values are rarely mentioned in daily life and
divorces occur with a frequency unknown in previous decades.
Even the paramount command that we should not harm anyone
goes unheeded. We need to renew our commitment to protecting
the dignity of every person and respect for life itself. Our parents

emphasized values they knew would outlive them. It is these values about which we need renewed dedication.

Our understanding of values grows as we attain adulthood. What we value may be a manifestation of how well our conscience is functioning. We cannot say conscience and values are identical, but it is difficult to comprehend the nature of values without first realizing how conscience reflects what we believe to be right and wrong. Values include ideals toward which we strive but do not fully achieve. A degree of self-consistency is essential for values to remain viable and serve as an internalized standard. To assume values remain static is an over-simplification. Conscience grows as we become more mature.

Wisdom

Wisdom is rarely discussed in professional journals. Chandler, Sternberg and Holliday are notable exceptions. These authors discuss reasons for the scarcity of treatises on this interesting and significant level of attainment. Wisdom must be included in appraisal of self-regulation processes. An illustration is the work of Baltes and Staudinger who are involved in studies which they refer to as the psychology of wisdom. Their theme is that wisdom has value beyond itself because it assists in understanding the power of the human mind.

This is also true of conscience, an equivalent to the attainment of wisdom. It is common to associate wisdom with utopia and to view its study as a waste of time. Investigation of this unique human quality, however, is one of the greatest avenues for gaining insight into our potential. Baltes and Staudinger define wisdom as "an expert knowledge system in the fundamental pragmatics of life permitting exceptional insight, judgment and advice involving complex and uncertain matters of the human condition" (p. 761). Central to this concept of wisdom is conduct, the interpretation and meaning of life, including knowledge about one's strengths and weaknesses, other people and society in general. A primary factor in attaining wisdom is the ability to integrate past and present experience and to relate what has been learned to prospects for the future. Feelings and cognitive abilities are involved. Baltes and Staudinger contend there is a close association between conscience and what they define as wisdom. Attainment of wisdom may not be possible without moral values, the process we designate as conscience.

Conscience and wisdom seem to follow similar paths developmentally, but it is through conscience that wisdom is revealed. As Fairlie observes, knowledge is essential for the highest level of function of both processes. He says, "If one is going to find oneself in oneself, one is well advised, before beginning the search in earnest, to make sure that one has put something inside which has made oneself worth discovering" (p. 106). His observation highlights that we live in a world not as it really is, but in the way we have caused it to be.

Science is an essential aspect of modern living, but it is not an infallible answer to all of life's struggles, stress, and pain. Science cannot provide the moral values for personal well-being and for peaceful, cooperative relationships with others. Awareness that there are no absolutes, except the virtues that counteract evil, causes some people to become cynical and depressed. Through wisdom we can refuse to be controlled by materialistic pursuits. Much of our suffering derives from over-secularization, putting us at risk for losing control of our destinies. Fairlie's observation is relevant. He says, "To celebrate our psychopathology, the abnormal as normal, the mad as sane, the schizophrenic as the whole, gets us no further than the loathing of humanity" (p. 137). Celebration of wisdom and attainment of internal moral values must not be neglected. If children do not know about moral values it is because we have not taught them what it means to be human and what it means to be accountable. Being accountable means taking responsibility for oneself. The price for lack of internalized moral values and self-control is beyond belief. We must face questions such as, will we realize children must have loving parents; will the forces that separate families be stronger than the forces that hold them together? Boorstin raises similar questions, "What baffles and frustrates us is that in this new kingdom—of computers, televisions sets, automobiles, airplanes, cellular phones, etc.— that we ourselves have made, we feel increasingly out of control" (p. 81). He makes another penetrating comment when he says, "We have created and mastered machines before realizing how they may master us" (p. 82). Behind these concerns is a new realization which emphasizes that conscience and wisdom are factors of our intellect that can be developed, are the basis of character, and provide awareness that virtue makes it possible to love ourselves and others. We cannot understand ourselves without understanding conscience. Wisdom and conscience are qualities that function throughout life. Some mental faculties, such as memory, show retrogression later in life but as Baltes and Staudinger have shown this is not true of wisdom. We have also found this is not true of conscience. It is fortunate that studies of conscience and wisdom are becoming more common. These basic processes are critical to the quality of life for people everywhere. As Erickson says:

> Indeed, any possible solution in terms of today's biggest threats to humanity would have to come to grips with the danger that human beings will become important manipulators in a technically perfect system of destruction and thus participate in the killing of millions of individuals without feeling mortally angry even at one. (p. 362)

The Wise

Sternberg summarizes four aspects of wise people: (1) they recognize that inherently difficult problems confront adults, (2) they have a comprehensive grasp of knowledge characterized by breadth and depth of understanding, (3) they recognize knowledge is uncertain and it is not possible for truth to be absolutely knowable at any given time, (4) they have a willingness and exceptional ability to formulate sound judgments in face of life's uncertainties (p. 7). Wisdom makes it possible to manage social institutions, to review one's life, and to introspect spiritually. A wise person searches for timeless and unchanging truths and is not content with the shifting phenomena of a material world. Sternberg admonishes that "the meaning contained in the concept of 'sin' may still be extremely relevant—indeed a matter of life and death" (p. 26). He also states that, "the wise individual is acutely sensitive to others' enjoyable growth experience" (p. 46). The wise person has ability to stimulate enjoyable self-discovery in others. Wisdom includes the ability to evaluate one's own life. A combination of inspiration and insight is effective in stimulating the growth of wisdom. Age alone is not an adequate criterion for defining wisdom. Baltes and Smith state that wisdom is "an expert knowledge system involving good judgment and advice in the domain, in the fundamental pragmatics of life" (p. 95). It has nothing to do with narrow forms of specialized expertise, but everything to do with a broader form of human understanding capable of cutting across unique particulars and arriving at a view that has the widest scope of possible applications. According to Sternberg a wise person has "knowledge about knowledge." He is comfortable with ambiguity, has sagacity, and engages in self-transcendence. He has learned from experience and is empathetic. He recognizes that it is not only knowledge itself that is important but how knowledge is used. He knows knowledge is fallible and that doubting is as important as knowing. Wisdom assumes a balance between knowing and doubting which is the foundation for a "wisdom atmosphere" (p. 208).

The wise person has resolved conflicts that arise from conscience and makes decisions about what is morally right. He combines experience, cognitive abilities, and feelings. He empathizes with the feelings of others, realizing that without a strong, working conscience there is floundering and lack of direction.

Holliday and Chandler suggest that a wise person is one who has done well in life, not necessarily in a material sense, but one who is able to embody principles of correct deportment. He exhibits exemplary understanding, including realization that it is dangerous to pursue technology and secularization without concern for moral values; he applies his knowledge in a social context. Emphasis on technological development alone leads to a narrow concept of human abilities and should not be construed as the whole of human knowledge. To adhere to the point of view that technical knowledge is all we need leads to ignoring wisdom, morals, and values. We have the potential for growing in wisdom as we become older but not everyone attains this level of knowing, although it is one of the greatest hopes we have in life. Growth in wisdom combines technical, practical, and self-reflective knowledge. Marcel says, "at the root of wisdom there is a degree of patience towards oneself which is the contrary of presumption" (p. 40). He also states that wisdom implies maturity, a respect for the past, and at least a veiled presence of the universal. He concludes, "The sage is in the first place one who has silenced his passions, or at least domesticated them; he is also independent of public opinion and prejudice and is able in all circumstances to resist the collective impulse" (p. 43).

Growth of ability to evaluate oneself parallels growth in wisdom. Behavioral scientists recognize the significance of wisdom in the study of the human mind including the study of conscience. It may be one of the greatest avenues for gaining insight into our endowments. Central to this concept of wisdom is interpretation of the meaning of life, including knowledge about one's strengths and weaknesses, other people and society. One's total personality and intellectual powers are involved. The attainment of wisdom is not possible without internal standards. Wisdom provides the basis for evaluation of experience and for relating it to the future.

Normal Conscience Development

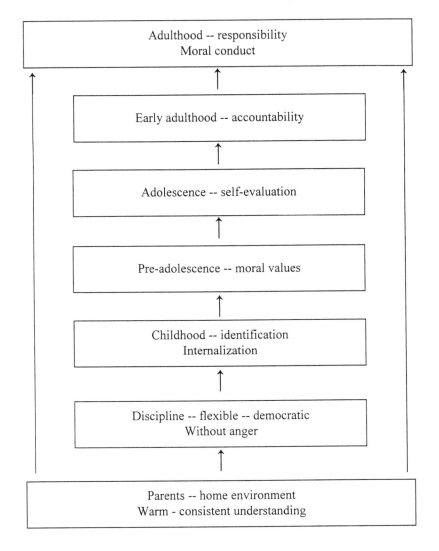

Figure One

CHAPTER II

Conscience Development

It is difficult to think of a process of greater consequence to happiness and survival than conscience, but because this fact is not realized its significance has been overlooked. This neglect is reflected by crime on the streets and glorification of violence in everyday life. Much remains to be learned but basic stages have been ascertained and serve as the background for child training. If this were done children would acquire the conscience they need for coping with the complex demands encountered in daily life.

The steps involved in conscience development are shown in Figure One. The first and most critical step is the emotional climate which pervades a child's family life. There is no more significant influence in the development of conscience. In Figure One we see that its development requires a warm, accepting, tolerant emotional environment characterized by patience and understanding. As shown in step two there must be a feeling of fairness, honesty, and flexibility together with an attitude which is not punitive. Relying on power and anger is devastating. The emotional framework must be one of patience and security if the child is to be successful at the next level, the step at which he internalizes the image of his parents. As he internalizes his parents' attitudes he also identifies with them, feeling they are trustworthy and that he can depend on them; his status is secure. These feelings of identification and internalization are the most crucial stages in emotional development and serve as the foundation for conscience.

At preadolescence the moral values developing since infancy form the basis for decision making, but the child is still dependent on external control. When he enters adolescence circumstances change, he must begin to assume responsibility for himself. He must engage in self-evaluation, a function of conscience. Children who enter this stage without having developed the level of arousal

27

required for self-control are vulnerable to criminality. The level of arousal is the basis for being sensitive to what is right, for what one should do. This level varies from person to person but everyone must attain the sensitivity necessary to maintain moral standards that guide and protect us from being victimized and from victimizing others. Even at this age self-evaluation requires the ability to make judgments based on moral standards. If these standards have not been established such judgments cannot be made. This level of control can be achieved only when levels occurring at earlier ages have been attained. Conscience is not suddenly in place, ready to provide arousal for adult living. It develops year by year so that when adulthood is attained it serves as the basis for moral decisions, whereby accountability takes on new meaning. No longer is one expected to need supervision. One's conscience serves as the guide. It is not age but ability to conduct oneself in a responsible way that determines one's level of maturity. Many people have lived long enough to be considered adults but their conscience development is only that of an adolescent or even younger.

There are ways in which we can help children, adolescents, and adults acquire a conscience. In psychology the term *conscience* is not often used. The phrase used is *moral development*. Damon emphasizes that being moral means we distinguish between good and bad and have a sense of obligation toward standards shared by the group in which we live; we have a concern for others and act responsibly on behalf of them. Emotional factors inherent in this behavior include empathy and self-esteem.

Morality and conscience are the result of parental guidance, supervision, and discipline. Parents must help their children learn the "rules" and this must be done in a way that does not injure the child's feelings. All aspects of daily life are involved, whether it be putting away toys, honesty in use of cars, avoidance of drugs, or hours for being at home. By two years of age children want information about what is permitted and what is not. In conscience training parental example is the most powerful force known. Showing anger and having temper outbursts is not the way to help children learn self-control. Threatening and punitive techniques do not foster conscience development. The most ineffective and, perhaps, the most damaging disciplinary pattern is inconsistency, at times being permissive and at other times using severe punishment. This pattern causes children to become aggressive and destructive. They do not acquire self-control because they learn the world is inconsistent, with a configuration of self- indulgence and violence. The most effective model for helping children develop conscience is one that follows democratic methods with restraint and patience without anger. Damon's work shows that democratic methods without control and control without democratic methods lead to disobedience, to lack of ability to use internal control. An authoritarian, punitive approach without warmth and understanding leads to poor self-regulation and poor inner-strength. Parents often use power to gain submission from children. This power approach means withdrawal of love. Love is given only when conformity is achieved. This is not the same as using warmth and understanding even when the child disobeys. Above all, parents must realize morality is not developed through immorality. Parents who manipulate and bribe their children, as occurs when love is used as a weapon, have children who attempt to gain success through manipulating others. This approach is a model for dishonesty, the opposite of integrity. Much of daily life involves living by rules, of being able to trust and recognize mutualness in a well-organized family and a sensitive society. Conscience shows we take obligations seriously, we want to live morally and accept responsibility for assisting others to do likewise. This involves the strength to be patient. Kirkegaard, the great philosopher who was deeply concerned about conscience, described patience as the courage which voluntarily accepts unavoidable suffering. We must help children learn that conscience is not a third party. It is "me" talking to "me". It is what makes me a person who makes decisions, the opposite of having peers make choices for me. We cannot be in control by following the crowd.

Schulman and Mekler make it clear that good behavior in children and adults is not attained by magic. Children are born with the unique capability for learning the difference between good and bad. But this matchless human quality must be developed. Children must be taught what is good and what is not. Only then can we expect them to attain self-control. A basic procedure through which such learning occurs is *internalization*. Although this psychological process is not fully understood it has been investigated extensively (Hersen and Last). Internalization means children identify with their parents and incorporate their feelings and attitudes. We can help our children internalize what we want them to learn through warmth, acceptance, and love. A "cold" attitude is demeaning, inhibits the internalizing process, and may cause children to internalize patterns of immorality and violence. Internalization is gained through a climate of love and understanding. It cannot be forced, but it can be enhanced by example. What is right must be taught, persistently and consistently. Rewards and bribes will placate children but will not teach self-control. When children feel rejected because they do not gain the approval of parents, they have difficulty internalizing what is right and wrong. It is through internalizing the feelings of others that children learn to empathize. Empathy is the basis for feeling the way others do, the basis for kindness. Parents need to show empathy for their children and understand when the child has guilt feelings, when he feels shameful or humiliated. There may be good reasons for the child's having these feelings and the parent's role is not to deny them. The child should be helped to understand why he feels as he does. These feelings derive from what he has done and he will learn to use self-control by acknowledging these feelings. Parents should be aware that love is much more beneficial than anger in the development of self-control.

Defiance and Aggression

Harris found abused children often become aggressive and hurt others. They begin to challenge their parents between the ages of two and three years. Between the ages of four and ten they begin to understand that their conduct leads to feelings of pride, shame, and remorse; they realize their feelings affect others and the feelings of others affect them. The more insecure they are the more vigilant they are of the feelings of those around them. The damaging effects of abuse, humiliation, and punitiveness are virtually inestimable and warrant greater understanding. Parents need to maintain empathy at all times. They must tolerate anger, anxiety, tantrums, and especially feelings of shame. Lavish compliments should be avoided because such expressions cause children to become anxious about living up to what is expected of them—needing to be perfect. Parents who are sympathetic listeners help children gain self-respect and identity.

Lytton, in a study of conduct disorders, found the most damaging influences for boys are absence of the father, absence of parental monitoring, and reasonable home control. Lowered self-control is part of the high risk syndrome. Hoffman also has shown that when the father is absent from the home boys do not develop a conscience normally. Choue, Johnson, Bowers, and Darvill found religious beliefs and practices foster the development of self-discipline, whereas permissiveness leads to poor self-control in adulthood. When children are given the attention they need and when discipline is used without hostility they develop a sense of security, belonging, and family.

Other investigators, notably Stilwell, Galvin and Kopta studied children from five to 17 years of age and found conscience was closely related to age. They concluded that conscience growth follows an invariant, hierarchical pattern of organization which should be evaluated in all children and adolescents who suffer from psychopathological disorders. Moreover, these investigators state that normal conscience development is critical as an approach to helping children and adults refrain from crime. Chazan indicates that behavioral scientists increasingly are providing evidence that moral values are influential in conduct. The controversial sex education programs have not reduced teen-age pregnancy nor promiscuity. Along with informational courses there must be specific instruction on moral values, on what is wrong and what is not. Values give meaning to what we do. Without these internalized meanings conduct is not changed.

Narramore studied conscience development from childhood to adulthood. Such development, he states, is central for both psychology and religion because when conscience remains at the punitive level it destroys self-esteem and leads to anxiety. Fraiberg showed that children who cannot identify with their parents or other care-givers are incapable of acquiring conscience. Sperry, a great behavioral scientist, believes free-will and determinism can be blended and that the assumption that these concepts present a paradox is in error. Both can be modified and integrated in a way that preserves moral responsibility. "By now," Sperry says, "it is widely agreed that what is needed to remedy our present self-destructive course is going to involve major changes world-wide in human thinking and behavior" (p. 883). Better science and technology are not the final solution according to Sperry, but "a possible

ray of hope in the outlook now is emerging—a new way of thinking
and perceiving that integrates mind and matter, facts and values,
and science and religion brings more realistic insights into the
kinds of forces that made the universe and created mankind" (p.
884). Conscience development involves the consideration of life
and death. As Leavy says, "As much as anything else, it is knowledge of death that defines our humanity" (p. 89). He also states that
overcoming temptation is the work of conscience. We will be more
successful in meeting our responsibilities as moral persons when
we recognize that education which provides only skills and information, without developing moral awareness, is inadequate.

Identification-Attachment

Evidence on how to assist children in developing a conscience
is growing. Kagan reports that attachment "conveys the idea that
the infant has acquired a special emotional relation with those who
care for him, and experiences pleasure or serenity in their presence but anxiety and distress when they are gone" (p. 129). He also
states, "identification is a major source of identity" (p. 136).
Bretherton and Waters have shown that children gradually build an
internal model of the person to whom they become attached. The
process of becoming attached relies on what is said and on how
one says it, as well as on the motivational regimen reflected by
example, encouragement, and support in the home. These investigators also found that children who develop good feelings of
attachment are less anxious, less vulnerable to daily disturbances,
and more secure in relationships. Identification builds self-worth
and these feelings influence how acceptable or unacceptable the
child feels himself to be in the eyes of those to whom he feels
attached. Feelings of insecurity result from lack of acceptance,
whereas shamefulness comes from rejection and contempt. A feeling of self-acceptance is the outcome of a well-developed conscience. Gaylin says "the primary emotions of cohesiveness are
guilt, shame, and pride, the essential components of the human
conscience"(p. 67). Children can be helped to feel that they are
attaining self-control, but a stable parenting family pattern is
essential. Reports show seventy percent of juveniles in correc-
tional facilities are from single-parent homes and three-fourths of
the girls from divorced parents see their fathers less than two days

per month. These girls are more likely to become sexually promiscuous, more often pregnant before marriage, and more often divorced if they marry. A happy home and childhood are significant influences in the lives of children.

Development From Within

Traditional study of child development has not been concerned with conduct as at relates to internal growth. As Freeman and Robinson emphasize, the constructs used have been too limited. They say, "development may be better conceived within individuals than across them" (p. 53); they stress the possibility of discovering new forms of development, new ways in which they might be fostered. This point of view is basic to the psychology of conscience. Conscience is rarely included in studies of emotional maturity and self-discipline. The traditional approach, however, is obsolete and has led to loss of shared moral values—the foundation for spiritual and psychological development, without which there is no standard on which contradictions faced in everyday life can be ordered. In the past we viewed psychological development as completed in late adolescence, all but eliminating the study of adult development. As Freeman and Robinson have noted, "our conviction is that it is of utmost necessity that we find a place for the concept of development in the study of adults" (p. 56). This emphasis is important to the concept of conscience growth because moral discernment is more than acquiring information about moral issues. It concerns the question of values, emotions, and goals. Development is not only a system of steps or events. It includes and is determined by desires, by what we hold to be most relevant. Ends are inherent. This is why interpretation of experience is necessary in the growth of understanding. What has been called "dissonance" is a part of this process because overcoming conflicts leads to achieving more ideal standards. Integration is necessary because behavioral change occurs only after new experiences have become a part of our being. New growth does not abolish the old. The new is integrated with the past, with internal standards that serve as the foundation for integration. Moreover conscience serves as the system through which experiences become assimilated. This process permits us to deepen life expe-

riences by managing the disruptions and disappointments that
sometimes impede the development of internal control.

Adolescence

Adolescence is a difficult time during which it is important for
parents to assist in understanding the role of conscience. In early
life control is under the direction of others, but as one becomes
older he must develop self-control; conduct is under the control of
internal standards. Following rules becomes self-directed. It is during adolescence that this transference from outer to inner control
becomes a central factor in growing up, in showing the strength of
one's conscience. What a significant period this is! Hersen and Last
have shown that 50% of youth who are antisocial in adolescence
engage in antisocial behavior as adults; they designate these individuals as having an "antisocial personality." This behavior is
observable between eight and ten years of age. These children are
self-centered, impulsive, manipulative, irresponsible, do not form
meaningful interpersonal relationships, and are lacking in feelings
of shame and guilt. They come from families where discipline is
inconsistent and punitive, where there is little family warmth and
cohesiveness, and where other family members have symptoms of
an antisocial personality.

Similar results are presented by Kendal. He classifies these
youth and adults as having disorders that are "externalizing" or
"internalizing," a step forward in understanding those whose conscience development has been neglected. He found that aggressive,
destructive conduct in early life leads to serious antisocial behavior later. These youth view the world as hostile and act accordingly; anger and self-control programs not only are necessary but
crucial. They can be helped to understand feelings such as anger,
depression, and hatred, as well as love and kindness. Development
of self-monitoring is critical to being able to live successfully.
Internalization in childhood cannot be overemphasized, but it is
only the beginning. Moral values must be fostered so that conscience is not only what parents have said but is the individual's
own system. Youth can say, "what is right is what I believe and
want to do." This is what transferring from outer control to self-
control means. As adults we must be able to say our conscience is
"the faculty within me which attaches itself to the highest that I

know, and tells me what the highest I know demands that I do"
(Chambers). As children grow into adolescence they become
aware that their parents are less than perfect. It is also a period
during which they may become rebellious, a manifestation of how
children go from hero worship to self-reliance. Nichols says this is
a period during which identity becomes consolidated, a time when
privacy should be respected, a time of much shame, of not wanting to be different, a time when self-love is paramount and defiance
expresses a need to grow.

Aronfreed, one of the pioneers in the study of conscience,
states that behavior has been internalized when it is no longer
dependent on external suggestions or restraints. Socialization is
not the same as internalization because it is dependent on external
forces. For behavior such as honesty to become stable, repetition
and example are required. Not until late adolescence should this
pattern be considered stable. It is also at this age that the cognitive
aspects of conscience are sufficiently developed so one can evaluate his behavior in terms of what is right and what is wrong. To do
so requires the ability to foresee consequences and to evaluate
them from the perspective of a value system. Everyone varies
between internal and external controls but conscience determines
whether good or evil is involved. Youth and adults whose value
organization is unstable are most vulnerable to suggestions from
peers or strangers and are most likely to ignore prohibitions. The
ability to be self-critical is of more importance in controlling one's
conduct than confession or apology because these depend on
social situations. Self-evaluation is for oneself and represents one's
ability to use internalized values. Children and youth rely on observation and imitation together with verbal explanations for internalizing values. In this way they become able to empathize, to be
altruistic, to engage in activities for the benefit of others without
expecting to receive something in return, to suppress inclinations,
and to conduct themselves in a moral way.

Gaining Self-Control

Effective discipline is the foundation for conscience development. To be most effective it should be immediate. It should not be
punitive but a process which helps the child learn to evaluate himself. Discipline is beneficial if the purpose is clear. Self-criticism

must be encouraged because it is the basis for self-guidance for a lifetime. A significant component of effective discipline is reparation because it serves as a means for establishing relationships between the parent and child. It is not only requiring confession or apology. Reparation means the child is required to make restitution; he gives back what he has taken. Paying back is necessary because corrective orientation implies that the child take responsibility for what has been done. In comparison, confession is less inclusive and may foster dependency. Fear, guilt, and shame almost always are involved but this is not necessarily detrimental because these feelings become a part of an effective conscience and are forms of internalized control, a part of self-evaluation. As Aronfreed observes, "The feelings of guilt, qualitatively, therefore, may be regarded as the feelings of anxiety that are attached to the harmful consequences of one's actions for others" (p. 247). Failure often brings guilt, especially when it brings shame to others. The child's conscience is expected to change, going through stages until at least late adolescence. But these changes do not occur in and of themselves. For conscience to develop normally there is constant need for suggestion and examples from everyday experience. This is the basis for developing a moral, value-oriented way of life. Values make up the system of internal monitors and are gained in much the same way as conscience. Children and youth gain and develop values through verbal instructions and a set of rules. Sometimes mild, common sense threats are involved but severe threats are not conducive to development of inner controls. The child must be able to understand what is expected. Severe discipline, if it is beyond the child's capacity to respond, is detrimental. Rejection and punitiveness damage the internalization process. A nurturing climate in the home and school is the most effective approach for the development of self-discipline. In our society TV often is used to control children's behavior. This interferes with gaining internal controls; it is also detrimental because children identify with TV characters who often represent violence. Ridicule, blame, and humiliation impede the internalization process. Moreover, those who have received physical punishment are aggressive toward others. However, the concept of conscience must include what being harmful means. Parents who are flexible about their children's development provide the most nurturing climate. Rigidity tells the child that he cannot improve. Parents who are flexible have set rules and follow them but they discuss all restraints with the child; they are not dictatorial. The children are given responsibility along with restraints. Flexible parents realize that conscience is formed through the experience of failure as well as all that happens in and outside the home. As stated by Baumeister (1991), "Our ancestors typically drew comfort from values that would outlive them" (p. 6). It is these values that must be conveyed to children and youth. Izard points out that a mature conscience involves more than simply negation, more than refusing to do evil. It is also choosing to do good. And, yes, sometimes this causes stress, loss of friends, and even the need to change a job. It may mean not being a member of the "gang." Only when we accept responsibility for doing what is right and do not fear being an example can we feel the exuberance which accompanies choosing to do good.

Klinger's study of meaning and incentives is closely related to conscience. His point of view is that without meaningful purpose we die. He believes our spirit can become sick and that incentiveness is crucial to well-being; life has meaning. He states "incentives control our behavior" (p. 291), which suggests that what we value most controls what we do. His position is that "the content of inner experience, in short, depends on the world of the person's incentives" (p. 62). The question which arises is whether incentives control conscience or does conscience control incentives. It is true that incentives and purpose dominate what we do. However, it is the role of conscience to monitor incentives if they are to conform to a moral way of life. We may have an incentive to be destructive and conscience must cause us to use self-control, not to victimize. We have seen that some people are so overridden with anxiety or depression that self-regulation becomes difficult. Conscience must have the strength to control our feelings including our incentives. It is not our belief that incentives control the self-regulatory system. Values, the basis of incentives, are learned through identification, bonding, imprinting, and instruction from childhood into adulthood. As life becomes more complex, the more complex the moral code must become if it is to provide guidance. In our era proclivities for immorality are rampant with dangers facing us all. However, this in no way means we are lost, that we cannot be moral and live humanely. As Hartman points out sanity and maturity require a moral ordering of life, a set of values to guide and sustain action. James also emphasizes the role of morality when he states, "on the one hand, moral responsibility, especially to the demands of truth, is the pinnacle of human maturity" (p. 2). The basic fact of moral behavior is that it requires us to be responsible, to live at the level of our highest potential. This moral psychology serves as our conscience. In helping children attain self-control we need to be aware that our desires often lead to immoral conduct. As Leavy observes:

> The root of neurotic pain lies in the fact that all sufferers distort their desires out of the basic human incapacity to fulfill them. To put it in the simplest form: because we cannot always have what we want, we pretend to ourselves that we want something else. (p. 65)

Emotional Disturbances

Progress is being made in understanding that emotional disturbances lead to conscience disorders in adolescents and in adults. An example is the work of Reynolds who suggests that emotional problems can be categorized as internalizing or externalizing disorders. This concept is useful when we analyze disorders of conscience because internalization is one of the most basic processes experienced by children and their families. According to Reynolds, the main internalizing disorders are anxiety, depression, psychosomatic involvements, eating disturbances, obsessing disorders, and mental illnesses such as schizophrenia. The externalizing disorders include hyperactivity, aggression, oppositional behavior, conduct disorders, and adjustment problems. Internalizing disturbances are experienced mainly inside with little evidence of them on the outside, whereas the externalizing disorders are of the "acting out" type and are apparent from observation. Those who have emotional problems of the externalizing type do not feel distress about their problems; self-monitoring is not well accomplished. But those having internalizing disturbances might suffer deeply, being conscious of their distress. As might be expected girls have more of the internalizing problems and boys more of the externalizing. Children having such problems have not bonded and identified satisfactorily. Sternberg studied the ways in which feelings of self-worth and competence might be associated. Children who underestimate their abilities are those who are low on feelings of self-worth. It is not difficult to see a relationship between low feelings of self-worth and feelings of hopelessness. Moreover, feeling competent and actually being competent also are related. When a child is preoccupied with the fear of failure he is not free to develop his potential. Some children become perfectionistic in attempting to cover their feelings of failure. Sternberg points out that contemporary psychology recognizes the self as an independent psychological structure that directs behavior, including self-regulatory patterns. Self-evaluation is mainly of two types, analysis on the basis of ideals and aspirations and on the basis of "oughts," the duties and obligations that we believe others have for us. Feelings of discrepancy are not necessarily the same as feelings of guilt. Self-discrepancy means that we are not living up to our aspirations or to the perceived expectations of others. When these feelings are out of hand we experience distress, shame, remorse, and depression. Children who feel that they are not living up to their parents' expectations sometimes feel abandoned. There is a connection between feelings of self-discrepancy and conscience. Self-worth, self-discrepancy, and self-regulation are components of conscience which operate at all of these levels and are significant factors in how we think about ourselves including the extent to which we feel competent. Beliefs about our capabilities are the basis of attainment. Children and adults with the same levels of ability perform differently, some successfully and some unsuccessfully. Self-worth and self-esteem are indicators of how we feel about ourselves and behind these is conscience. Unless it is well-developed many pitfalls can be expected. When we feel competent, we can say, "this is what I know is right, this is what I will do about it." We are not worrying about what should be done. Our cognitive abilities are free to pursue goals because we know we are competent.

We hear students say, "I have values of my own but I don't think I should judge what others do; that's their business." This attitude avoids responsibility. We should be honest and expect others to be honest. What about kindness? Is this feeling irrelevant? What about harming others? Do we condone rampant violence? What about duty, responsibility and obligation? The person with a mature conscience realizes these are value judgments that will live

on long after we are gone. Morals are more than personal preference, as discussed by Wallach and Wallach (1990). Values are not
only subjective opinions, they are the principles which make life in
society possible. Baumrind says, "All human action has a moral
dimension . . . the individual's rights are inseparable from his or her
responsibilities to the community" (p. 256). She observes further
that we as individuals are responsible for our own lives, we are
required to take charge of our actions, to answer to ourselves and
to the community for the consequences of what we do. We are
social beings and do not belong only to ourselves. We cannot be
respectful without considering the well-being of others. In so doing
we do not deny or eliminate self-interest; rather self-interest is
incorporated into virtuous conduct. Baumrind states that "my
worth as a moral agent rests on the adequacy of my judgments and
actions" (p. 272). It is we as individuals who determine moral standards. Groups may help some persons to discover what is right, but
right is not determined by consensus. Group judgments often serve
to destroy individual responsibilities by diffusing personal-moral
standards. Again, to quote Baumrind:

> the moral maturity of an individual in a society can be evaluated
> by how little his or her conduct is governed by the hedonic cal-
> culus, and is motivated instead by an overriding regard for inte-
> grating personal development as a moral agent and commitment
> to a realizable ideal of the common good. (p. 276)

The processes involved in conscience development are shown
graphically in Figure One. Discipline is the beginning point. It is
also the primary source for disorders of conscience because poor
discipline leads to confusion of what is right and wrong. This confusion usually results in disturbed, aggressive conduct by eight to
ten years of age.

Internalization

Perhaps the most important processes in conscience development are identification and internalization. Identification precedes
internalization because the child feels a parental bond. It is precisely this process that leads to conscience development. The child
incorporates right and wrong through his parents' discipline and

the attachment he forms to them. Conscience development may be arrested or impeded at any level. If internalization and identification are disturbed, conscience disorders should be expected. Those who at adolescence and early adulthood are conscienceless are victims of being unable to identify with what is right and wrong. In the normal development of conscience internal standards are established in the pre-adolescent period, from about eight to ten years of age. This vital period in the development of moral conduct is recognized by many authorities, especially those involved in the study of criminality. This age span is most critical for boys because at this age "acting-out" behavior becomes apparent and troublesome. Hersen and Last have shown that boys who show aggression and poor self-control at this age that often become delinquents or criminals when they are older. There is little question that if we are to gain control of violence on the street it is at this age our efforts must be focused. Aggressive children must be given special attention because of their potential for becoming violent adults.

Adolescence is the period during which the child progresses from outside supervision to self-control. It is a difficult period, but when developmental periods have gone well children go through it without distress. If the earlier stages have been disturbed, adolescence may be overwhelming. Parents should be aware that adolescents need special support to understand the demands of adulthood and being confronted with the need to make choices for themselves, an experience which is often frightening. Without taking over and making choices for them, parents can suggest and be supportive, especially with moral questions. At this age relativism, rationalization, and peer pressure become critical and need to be discussed. There is no reason to avoid questions of right and wrong. Adolescents are responsive when given an opportunity to express themselves freely.

The last stage in conscience development is early adulthood, another vital period in attaining concepts of moral value. But conscience development does not cease as we become adults. If circumstances are favorable it develops throughout the life span. However, there is a period during which moral standards are being established and this includes the period of early adulthood. Many new experiences are encountered including exposure to distrust, dishonesty, and expectation levels not previously recognized. Early adulthood is a stressful period for young people not only because of new demands, but because of the confusion about what is wrong and what is right. One of the most common issues raised by young adults is "what do they expect from me?" Along with this question is the expectation that "now I must be accountable." Many questions of responsibility are not realized until early adulthood. These questions are made more complex by society because of mixed guidelines for moral conduct. We condone activities by placing them in a "gray" area—"if you can get by with it, do it." Hence, early adulthood is a period during which conscience development is established or ignored as the guide for conduct.

Conscience and Obedience

It is difficult to understand conscience without considering obedience. Kelman and Hamilton raise a fundamental question when they discuss "crimes of obedience." They define this behavior by stating that it "deals with the consequences that often ensue when authority gives orders exceeding the bounds of morality or law" (p. xi). The issue is why some persons show unquestioning obedience and show no resistance to unjust authority. Why is it that under certain conditions moral obligations and convictions become weakened? Kelman and Hamilton identified three processes: authorization, routinization, and dehumanization. Through authorization some individuals feel that their personal responsibility is relinquished; they do not need to make moral choices. Routinization does not provide opportunity for making moral choices nor raise questions about them, as occurs in government, business, medicine or elsewhere. In dehumanization persons as persons no longer exist so morality is avoided. "Crimes of obedience are immoral acts committed in response to orders or directives from authority" (p. 307). Crimes committed in the name of authority are increasing in number and in the depth of cruelty involved, as witnessed in ethnic wars, wars of annihilation, and the behavior of gangs. Any bureaucratic organization might be dangerous insofar as providing opportunities for committing crimes of obedience. Every individual faces the choice to obey or disobey. There are limits to power and we avoid moral values to our own defeat. Persons who are value-oriented are more likely to challenge immoral authority. If we are value-oriented we focus on conduct which leads to recognition of responsibility. As Kelman and

Hamilton point out, "perhaps societies and organizations will increasingly learn that fostering value orientation among their numbers, although it entails short-term costs, can contribute to their long-term stability" (p. 338). Mixon also stresses the dangers of crimes of obedience. In discussing the history of obedience he emphasizes its role in the development of civilization. To be subordinate is to always be faced with the need to question those in authority, even at the risk of alienating them. We cannot subscribe to authorized crime, to what Mixon fears as the normality of evil. This concept of acceptance of evil is one of the most fundamental issues we face in modern society. To be neutral and overlook evil is a danger with vicious consequences. When we become aware of evil practices, no matter where, it is essential that we adhere to moral values. There cannot be a conscience for private lives and another that relinquishes more responsibility in business and professional lives. Moral conduct knows no borders; it is the basis of behavior no matter what the circumstances, public or private.

Kroy points out that conscience has an imperative role in open societies. Milgram's work (1974) provides insights into why conscience is sometimes turned off. He has shown that when outside authority is adhered to our inner control system may not operate. It is as though when an authority sets the rules (an army officer, a business executive, or a cult figure), one's individual conscience is overrun. Milgram's findings provide insight into the mass behavior that made the Holocaust possible. In recent years we have observed religious groups, under the authority of "God," commit horrendous violence toward those not affiliated with their particular beliefs. The reason for human beings relinquishing inner control to an authority perceived as being above themselves and thus becoming capable of inhuman behavior is not clear. This is an area of conduct that has been largely overlooked. Nevertheless, this behavior may be only an extreme example of what we have suggested is common at a less severe level. Many individuals have what might be designated as two consciences, one for public life and one for private life. Almost daily we observe influential, powerful individuals display uprightness in public, but then someone victimized by them speaks out and we discover they have been outrageously corrupt in their private lives.

In seeking power individuals may exceed the boundaries of morality, as do some superiors in business, government, and medicine, and others who are leaders in society. When given orders some people relinquish moral standards and obey "superiors" even when the orders are cruel, restrictive, or criminal in intent. Such conformity is a primary factor in street gangs and drug cartels. This relinquishment of self-control is not easy to explain, but for certain individuals it seems to be easier to accept external control than to maintain self-regulation. All authority is subject to limitations. No matter who gives the orders their intent must be evaluated.

Conscience and Authority

Crimes committed in the name of authority by individuals and groups are growing. It is not uncommon to read about anti- and pro-abortion groups committing violence on behalf of what they believe is right. It appears that when people become "members" of a group some become role-players. When this happens they no longer feel personal responsibility for what they do. We must foster value orientations and make it clear that these values are to be adhered to no matter what circumstances confront us. We should study the conditions under which certain individuals find it easy to forego the warning they receive from conscience, and moral obligations become weakened. Roof found the "baby boomers" deplore what has happened in our society. He quotes one of those interviewed as saying "right and wrong is right out the window. Everything is choice" (p. 104). Roof concludes "contemporary pluralism demands spiritual models of tolerance and openness, which at the same time encourages principles of integrity and conviction" (p. 246). An immoral conscience always believes its convictions are right.

No problem that relates to crimes of obedience is more evident than the one found in cults. In recent years we have witnessed the horrors of hundreds of people being victimized because of their following a leader capable of betraying them to his own advantage. The leaders themselves must be viewed as having a sick conscience, often to the extent of being mentally ill. But what about their followers? Our interest in them and in cultism concerns the role of conscience. We have stated that an emotional disturbance can override the conscience process. In the case of cultists we see an example, albeit sometimes bizarre, of how emotional turmoil destroys the workings of conscience. It may be that those who become members of cults never had a normal conscience or it may be punitive so they are conscience ridden and have a need for "authority" to make "right and wrong" decisions for them. They have disorders of conscience. Wolf quotes Thomas Jefferson as saying, "I know no safe depository of the ultimate powers of the society but the people themselves—the people themselves have the ability to handle that power, trusting our leaders to do what is right, but trusting in ourselves to know what 'right' really means" (p. 15).

Comic strip cartoonist Bill Keane had an insightful comment in *Family Circus* when he had one child telling another, "conscience is like Mommy tellin' you not to do somethin' but she isn't there." This illustrates the process of internalization and reveals how conscience operates at a young age. Ketcham in one of his *Dennis the Menace* episodes revealed another aspect of conscience when he had Dennis tell his mother, "My conscience told me not to do it, but I decided to go along with Tommy's conscience instead," which illustrates the problem of what happens when children, youth, or adults give in to peer pressure. There is no alternative to following one's own conscience, no matter what the circumstances. Often we expect institutions to establish what is right so that we need not take responsibility for making these decisions, failing to recognize that schools, churches, and government are made up of individuals. If we do not promote what we know to be right, there is little any organization can do about it. We must be ready and willing to foster conscience development in ourselves and others. If we recognize this challenge and become disciples for good versus evil it will lead to reformation of society. Mixon says, "If the object is to produce a conscience that will identify authorized criminal commands as wrong, then the essential thing to be grasped and believed is that it is always wrong to harm and kill. Most people do not believe that this is so and do not teach it to their children" (p. 131).

One cannot consider the function of conscience without including its relationship to obedience. Conscience serves as an authority that asks us to recognize our motives as being morally right or wrong. But conscience is not the only authority we must deal with. Everyone faces some form of authority no matter what his role. Law enforcement people, military personnel, religious and political leaders illustrate how through our organizations and agencies we have authority figures throughout our social structure. We need such persons. The question we raise pertains to how individuals regard authority, the extent to which we might follow dictates of those in authority without using our conscience to evaluate the orders.

Conscience must be functional at all times to alert us to what is immoral even though it might be an order from a superior. If we relieve ourselves from using self-evaluation and give up our judgment, following only what those in authority say, the result may be committing crimes of obedience, sometimes even on a national basis. We must be cognizant that unless conscience functions normally we will relinquish personal judgment in favor of what authorities say even though what is suggested is injurious to ourselves and to others.

Obedience itself is related to internalized standards. If these standards are vague and confused we are more likely to commit crimes of obedience. Only when conscience tells us that the behavior is immoral can we refuse to be victimized. This is the basis for the decision to follow or not to follow orders, no matter how prominent or prestigious the source of the order might be. One factor is peer pressure. People often do not realize how they are influenced by the opinions of relatives and associates. While their comments might be helpful, it is imperative that we reserve decision making for ourselves. In so doing we maintain self-control and do not relinquish responsibility, an essential aspect of not being victimized by crimes of obedience. Sometimes we find ourselves defying those in authority. If this means our defiance is focused on those who have cause to harm us the issue becomes difficult. But it might be that at these times we must be aware of the arousal we receive from conscience and without anger proceed on the basis of these messages. To give in to immorality leads only to more difficult questions and to self-destructive trends. Each of us, no matter what our role, must assume responsibility for helping others as well as ourselves to realize that crimes of obedience are prevalent everywhere and, therefore, conduct ourselves on the basis of our own standards. We will comply and obey only when the conduct involved is not in disagreement with our internalized moral values. Authorization from others, no matter what position they hold, does not mean the behavior involved is what we believe to be morally appropriate. We cannot allocate moral responsibility. If we do it is as though we have no conscience. We must maintain self-control under the jurisdiction of our conscience whether orders are given by individuals, government agencies, religious leaders, or gang and cult leaders. Crimes of obedience are common and sometimes the cruelty is unbelievable. We are especially vulnerable to such criminal behavior when we stand to gain from the judgments and decisions involved. We are prone to overlook harming others when the outcome is to our advantage, politically or otherwise. Our well-being is dependent on our not relinquishing judgment or self-control to others. Only we should make judgments about what we will do. Behind these judgments is conscience.

Self-Criticism

Conscience requires us to be accountable. When we do not hold ourselves accountable we should expect trouble. Those who have a mature conscience avoid problems because they have an understanding of their past actions and feelings of obligation for their behavior in the future. They are capable of self-criticism, the essence of conscience. Self-criticism involves blameworthiness, but properly blaming oneself is part of maturity. It means we take responsibility for our conduct. Self-criticism entails feeling of shame, remorse, and guilt. These feelings are part of a normally functioning conscience albeit at times they may be excessive and require remedial assistance; overcontrol can be as debilitating as underdevelopment. Though similar in certain ways, guilt and shame differ. Feelings of shame are experienced when there are onlookers, real or imagined. An audience is not assumed for feelings of guilt. Loevinger observes:

> A complete understanding of the phenomena of so rich and varied an experience as conscience may be impossible. One additional element of a mature conscience must be added, however: disinterestedness. A person with a truly mature conscience has the possibility, even the proclivity if not to love others exactly as he loves himself, at least to take their standpoint into equal account with his own. This involves treating others as ends rather than as means, but more than that. It means transcending both egocentrism and the orientation that allows conscience to be satisfied by mere obedience. (p. 271)

Loevinger also stresses that in infancy and early life the begin-
nings of conscience are unpleasant because restriction and discipline are necessary. The child must accept these restrictions to
maintain a relationship with his parents. Standards of what is right
and wrong are conferred on him as he goes through a period of
conformity. When properly disciplined a child gains the ability to
evaluate himself. As he does so he must integrate feelings of
shame, remorse, guilt, aggression, and anger because these serve
as the basis for conscience. Through such growth he becomes forgiving, tolerant of his own feelings, and the attitudes of others.
Only those having a mature conscience can "love their neighbors
as themselves." They have incorporated moral standards of the
highest order and attained a significant level of mental and emotional development, including the ability to conceptualize the
nature of moral values. Only then can we value others, see them as
persons who may be different but who have rights of their own
even though their opinions vary from ours. This highest level of
humanness goes beyond mere conformity. It is a realization that we
are members of a society. What we expect and desire must not
come at the price of jeopardizing love for others. A conscience that
seeks only to obey cannot function at this level; it represents
arrested development. Again we find the conclusion by Loevinger
insightful. She says, "The conformist stage is reached by most but
no means by all children. Growth beyond this stage is problematic,
with diminishing numbers ever reaching successively higher
stages" (p. 289). She explains:

> Self-administration of sanctions, self-evaluation, and self-selec-
> tion of the rules to be followed. Ideals having reference to a
> wider social unit than one's immediate family are characteristic.
> The obligation to conform to rules, regardless of consequences
> of one's actions for others. Interpersonal relations move beyond
> cooperation and reciprocity to a deeper mutuality. (p. 290)

Conscience growth is a progressive process in which external controls become less necessary. Many people do not achieve this level
of conscience development, the level at which conscience is free
of guilt, has tolerance for ambiguity, and ability to adjust to daily
life.

Conscience and Beliefs

Conscience entails beliefs which form a major part of the psychology of right and wrong. As self-discipline is attained, one also develops points of view, a belief system. Conscience reflects what one believes to be of value. According to Kegan, we organize our experiences to gain meaning. This is how moral values become established. Kegan refers to this process as "meaning making," the basis of beliefs fundamental to successful living. The concept of meaning-making needs to be reinforced in as many ways as possible, in schools, churches, and in the courts. Youth are not identifying with the meanings we propose. One reason is that we do not have clear meanings in mind when we go about our daily lives. To be a meaning-maker is to be a model of the kind of person we want to be. We take moral values seriously because they are meaningful when integrated with experience. The more we assist others to gain meaning the more we fulfill our role as meaning-makers.

Taggart points out that superstitions are a type of belief system which may become threatening to entire societies, emphasizing that everyone has a belief system. Beliefs serve as an integrating "philosophy" in mediating daily existence. She states, "belief systems are constructs of the human imagination that enable us to cope with the terrors and opportunities of self-awareness" (p. 19). We think and act on the basis of our beliefs. If we think that all is relative and that moral standards are useless, we will conduct ourselves accordingly. Secularism is a belief system of which science is a part. A comprehensive belief system incorporates relativism and science and includes moral beliefs which serve as the foundation for character.

Colby and Damon have shown the importance of moral values in all aspects of life. They found that people who made a moral commitment had a pattern of (1) disregard for risk with a disavowal of courage; (2) a certainty of response in matters of principle; (3) an unremitting faith and positive attitude even under the worst of circumstances; (4) taking direction and gaining support from those they served and inspired; (5) being dynamic in facing change and maintaining continuity (p. 293). This pattern can be seen as the utmost of what conscience development means and illustrates the significance of moral belief systems. Through research in theology, education, psychology, and psychiatry we are beginning to realize the practical significance of moral beliefs.

People who have moral courage make a difference. Relativism is seriously deficient as a belief system and does not foster character development.

Much can be learned about the growth and function of conscience through the study of beliefs. We have mentioned the work of Dummelow in which he describes how conscience came to Adam and Eve. There are differences in the concept of conscience as found in the Old and New Testaments. Much evil pervades our world, but only human beings have the capability of making this observation. Only with the ability to be moral can evil be recognized. There is reason for concern about whether we really care deeply about the moral standards that make us aware of the evil surrounding us.

The sexual revolution has not resulted in greater understanding. The sex education movement failed largely because reference to moral values was incidental. Moreover the practice of couples living together before marriage has not reduced the divorce rate. In fact the incidence of divorce has increased, as has the incidence of abortions and illegitimate births. No-fault divorce also resulted in an increase in the divorce rate. If we are to be serious about these issues we cannot ignore the role of conscience and the need to bring conscience training to the forefront in the home, church, school, government, and business.

Through the work of professionals such as Bostrum we learn that conscience development is a significant factor in alerting us to the rules we want to live by individually and as a society. He points out that "we are moral creatures, not because we are so good, but because we have the capacity to examine questions of 'should' and 'ought' and 'the good'" (p. 284). He raises the question of whether conscience can be trusted to give us direction for the choices we make. Conscience can function only to the extent it has been developed. We have mentioned it can be underdeveloped or overdeveloped. In either case it is not functioning normally and does not serve as a dependable guide. We have referred to Eigen's work on the "immoral conscience." This designation emphasizes that it is not uncommon to encounter people who are unable to be sensitive to what is right and wrong. This does not mean we should denigrate the importance of conscience as a guide for moral conduct. Rather, the question of whether conscience can be dependable must be considered in relation to the extent that it has been developed in each of us.

Bostrum emphasizes how conscience growth has varied and changed over the centuries. He shows that in Old Testament times rules were given by God from the outside. But we must not conclude that the concept of right and wrong is lacking. There is a great deal about morality in the Old Testament, with reference to shame, remorse, self-esteem, and awareness of evil. A related concept of interest to the study of conscience is found in Ecclesiastes when the writer admonishes his son by saying, "My son, be modest in your self-esteem, and value yourself at your proper worth" (10:28-31). In our generation there is overwhelming emphasis on helping children and adults to have high self-esteem. The writer reminds us that overvaluation of ourselves can be disastrous. Unrealistic feelings of self-esteem are related to problems of immorality or an otherwise poorly developed conscience. This can be seen in what has been referred to as functional atheism, a belief system that professes that "everything is under my control." Values and spiritual strength are ignored and life becomes a struggle for power and advantage. As a belief system this is dangerous because it leads to dysfunctional families, poor value orientation, immorality, violence, and addiction.

The term conscience is used in the New Testament. St. Paul assumes that those to whom he writes have a conscience and that its function is to serve as a moral guide. In 1st Corinthians 10:25 and 10:27 he admonishes people about having weak consciences because they are unduly concerned about what they eat instead of about the spiritual aspects of their lives. He distinguishes between the human voice within and God's voice, a distinction which is significant because it gives conscience status, emphasizing its relation to religious beliefs.

The Role of Conscience

Studies in psychology and psychiatry sometimes lead to skepticism regarding the purpose of conscience. As Granrose suggests, "some schools of psychology, especially psychoanalysis, have given many persons the impression that they have 'explained away' conscience" (p. 3081-A). The difference between a mature conscience and a weak, immature one is whether its messages are accepted critically or uncritically. The role of conscience is to integrate feelings, purposes and intentions, to reflect decisions on the basis of the total circumstances involved, not arbitrarily, childishly, or in mere conformity. Granrose refers to this inner-cognitive process as "consulting your conscience" (p. 3081-A). It has not been denied in religious circles, but it has been neglected through secularization of religious traditions and doctrines. The New Testament has much to say about the role of conscience in our daily lives. In Acts 24:16 Paul says, "This being so, I myself always strive to have a conscience without offense toward God and men." This statement has profound implications. Paul is not indifferent toward his conscience. He strives to keep it active in a way that will not offend God or others. He strives to be at peace with his conscience.

Another example is from John 8:9, which states, "then those who heard it, being convicted by their conscience, went out one by one, beginning with the oldest, even the last. And Jesus was left alone, and the woman standing in his midst." This passage follows the admonition by Jesus that those who had not sinned should cast the first stone. This too has profound implications for the meaning of conscience. Jesus was aware that everyone has a conscience; it is basic to everyone's conduct, including the fact that no one has a perfect record in doing what is right. Jesus used this knowledge to teach his accusers of their own hypocrisy. His accusers were telling him he was wrong to speak to an immoral person when He was preaching about the moral life and what it means. So Jesus gave them an opportunity to show their own morality by saying if you have never committed a wrong (sin) then go ahead; show it by taking it out on a person who has been immoral. At this point a significant happening occurred. Every one of his accusers walked away knowing they could not live up to the request made by Jesus. How did they know this? They were made aware of their hypocrisy through their conscience. As the passage says, "being convicted by their conscience." There are times when conscience convicts us because the situation in which we find ourselves is obviously wrong, but until conscience calls it to our attention we are not aware of our hypocrisy and that what we were about to do is in opposition to our beliefs, values, faith, and hopes. This work performed by conscience is also demonstrated by Timothy 4:2 in which he says, "speaking lies in hypocrisy, having their own conscience seared with a hot iron." In this passage too, the behavior involved concerns hypocrisy or conduct which is opposite from integrity. Timothy emphasizes that hypocritical acts have their own price because the result is a conscience that burns like a hot iron. Most of us have had such experiences.

We have observed that conscience and soul are not the same. We are born with an innate ability to develop a conscience however, it must be formed through teaching and the example of parents, other adults, and peers. This point of view is not in conflict with religion but some people cling to the idea that conscience is the voice of God. What we have been given is the capacity to develop the ability to distinguish between right and wrong. As human beings we are above lower animals and have the freedom to choose and to make moral judgments. We are unique and it is up to us to take responsibility for developing conscience. Faith and belief serve to underscore reality. Extreme beliefs and fanaticisms are life distorting as seen in cults and mass movements to annihilate others. Internalized beliefs make sense out of a chaotic world. A strong faith provides the basis for coping despite uncertainty. Neurotic religion is a form of thought control. Our beliefs must remain open to contradiction and mystery, to the unknown. Healthy belief transcends helplessness. It is easy to think of ourselves as good people who need not worry about conscience. We know we are not perfect, but through what we think is tolerance and acceptance we condone evil. We do not discriminate between honesty and dishonesty, the level at which we accept corruption as being normal; it becomes a gray area with relativism overrunning conscience.

Jones (1994) argues brilliantly for recognition of the fact that religious beliefs and science are not contradictory when he states, "science and religion are related human attempts to make sense out of a very complex existence" (p. 189). Religion provides a means for ordering our lives and enhancing the conscience process. Jones also suggests that "contemporary philosophy of science does not support a radical or categorical separation of science from other forms of knowing, including religious knowing or belief" (p. 188). Value neutrality is impossible. We should recognize that one cannot be intimately involved in the fundamental issues of our lives without considering moral and religious beliefs.

However, as Butt says, "In a world enamored with science, the word *belief* does not carry much respect compared with the word *fact"* (p. 115). He suggests that society's need to believe in scientific neutrality is so inherent it supersedes all other approaches in public affairs so issues cannot be anything but secular. If it is not secular it is demeaned as only personal opinion. Virtually all aspects of public life, including education, have replaced religious and spiritual aspects with secular concepts and rules.

Conscience and Feelings

Conscience must be considered together with emotional, spiritual, and mental development. There are those who cannot achieve conscience growth because of mental limitations or mental diseases such as schizophrenia. There are also individuals who after attaining a normal conscience lose it through brain diseases such as Alzheimer's. However, the greater problem is how conscience is altered by feelings such as anger, shame, guilt, hate, and rage. When we become angry or when we have temper outbursts, we are not responsive to conscience. Anger is a powerful feeling. Only when we have effective self-regulation can such feelings be controlled.

Any emotional outbreak might override messages from conscience. The messages have not gone away. They have been overcome by feelings that control what we do. We should be aware that there are times when we lose control and do not respond to our conscience as we should. Sometimes these experiences are normal. It is when we have a pattern of letting anger, jealousy, or hatred dominate us that it precludes loving relationships and prevents feelings of achievement at home or at work. There are other ways in which conscience development is obstructed. These include addictions to drugs and alcohol, eating disorders, and smoking. These unhealthy life patterns involve conscience. When self-regulation is understood and moral values predominate, destructive patterns can be controlled and a more advantageous lifestyle established.

Love, Guilt, and Identity

A mature conscience can be achieved only in relation to one's ability to love others. Jesus explained how this can be done when he said "love your neighbors as yourselves." He did not say we should simply love ourselves which would be narcissistic selfishness. Nor did He say we should simply love others which might lead to self-destruction. Rather, we should love ourselves to the same extent we love others. If we are guilt-ridden, shameful, and remorseful, we cannot love ourselves properly, our self-esteem is low, we are dissatisfied, angry, and cynical. A punitive conscience causes us to be angry at ourselves. An immature conscience causes us to constantly find fault in others; we cannot respect and trust others. When our conscience disorder is alleviated we can feel the power of love. We realize love is wanting good for everyone and no longer blame ourselves for "not doing enough" for our family.

Often we esteem people for who they are rather than for what they have done. According to Baumeister (1991), "Instead of offering people firm answers about what is right (or/and) wrong, society offers an assortment of possible views and allows people to pick and choose among them" (p. 115). In other words we have become more and more permissive. Picking and choosing is part of the privilege of living in a democracy. But moral values are a part of the privilege of being free. Without them we have decadence. Morality is power that counters self-indulgence and irresponsibility. Moral values provide purpose and meaning through which we achieve feelings of self-worth. Values are the basis for shared meanings and purposes.

Guilt is a significant aspect of suffering. Perhaps more people suffer from guilt than from physical pain. It occurs when what we do causes us to give up on higher levels of value. When this occurs we might seek relief through alcohol and other drugs. When guilt feelings are not relieved it is common to experience what Baumeister (1991) refers to as a "meaning vacuum" (p. 246). This suffering is caused by a disordered conscience and the outcome takes the form of relinquishing feelings of right and wrong and behaving as though moral values do not exist. But guilt is a source of information. Jacques explains, "it is this feeling of guilt, or conscience, that is so fundamental to our capacity to become social beings . . . the basis of social concern lies in the capacity for guilt which results from internal conflict" (pp. 168-178). Conscience is not only a filter, it serves as the center for judgment. Meaning assumes a type of permanence which is dependent on conscience. That which is good and upright does not change from one era to the next. This is why values such as honesty, respect, and love are

the basis for human relationships, as represented by a mature conscience. Meaning is always involved. Everyday experiences must
be integrated into a pattern that serves as a guide for decisions and
orientation. Essentially this is the process of meaning-making. It is
when our experience becomes disengaged and no longer meaning-
fully associated with the past that we lose identity.

The pattern of our age is that we are struggling, some of us
almost desperately, to find meaning on which we can depend, not
realizing it is moral values that provide meaning throughout the
world. Without these values we face chaos no matter which political party is in power or what the economy is like. Psychological
analysis shows that in this era, as moral structure weakened we
lost identity; we did not know who we are. As a result we have an
avalanche of books, programs, and therapy sessions to tell us who
we are, to fill our meaning vacuum, to help us define ourselves, and
to help us gain identity. Sadly many of these approaches have
failed because of superficiality. They lack a belief in what is right
and what is wrong. Our culture is saying, "you are free to choose
anything you want if it makes you feel better." Values are only what
we think is fun, what provides immediate pleasure, what we accept
on the basis of feelings. But the search for identity is relieved only
when we realize that self-indulgence does not relieve guilt, help us
understand shame, give us an identity based on values nor provide
the basis for a mature conscience. Wallach and Wallach (1983)
state, "Our society seems to value assertion or expression of self
as an ultimate good" (p. 13). These authorities also believe "people
can find significance in what they do because of its meaning for
others" (p. 3). They conclude that our pattern is to look out for ourselves first; "self-concern is a dominant cultural theme" (p. 11).
Contributing to the well-being of others, pursuing that which is of
value outside of ourselves is crucial to gaining a mature identity.
Conscience is our own voice, not the voice of someone else. It is
the voice of our deepest being asking us to be what we can be and
live up to our potential. Egotistical patterns for living are detrimental to the development of conscience; spiritual factors cannot
be ignored. Restraints are inherent for our own good as well as for
the good of others.

Emphasis on freedom to satisfy our ego may be contrary to
gaining a sense of meaning. Conscience is the system that restricts

putting ourselves first and requires that we supersede selfishness. According to Wallach and Wallach (1983):

> Such conduct includes primary concern for other people rather than oneself, making commitments to service and sacrifice for others' sake and abiding by these commitments rather than attending to one's own sense of gratification and an attitude of forgiveness rather than ventilation of hostility toward those who cause us distress. (p. 230)

It is in doing good we restore ourselves, what having purpose beyond ourselves means. Only rarely is conscience understood for what it is, a process which integrates other abilities. Kroy, in his volume *The Conscience, a Structural Theory*, states that "one needs a conscience in order to be a possible member of an open society—membership in an open society presupposes the capacity of applying one's conscience to one's intentions" (p. 161).

We stress the importance of helping children attain a fully developed, stable, working conscience year by year. We want them to have the best education possible, but knowledge of history, English, physics, and math is not enough; these are means to an end, not an end in themselves. We must teach what the purpose of life really is: to serve others, to show integrity, to love our neighbors as ourselves. This requires more than skills and secular knowledge. It means that we teach the nature of spiritual values, the basis of a mature conscience, and realize that in being examples we can expect youth to "change the world." Because there are many single parent families, there is a need for grandparents and other adults to assist in providing examples of everyday integrity. We do not wait for others to provide role models, we do this ourselves as morally responsible persons. We demonstrate what it means to have a conscience. We make it clear that what Toffler calls "a throw away society" (p. 47) is not the world we want to foster. It is not the society we are capable of developing.

CHAPTER III

Self-Control

We have referred to conscience as a self-regulation system. Historically some psychologists resisted the premise that inner feelings are the primary basis for conduct. Nelson (1993), one of the investigators who helps us understand that there is a self-regulation system, says it is this process "that works to keep an individual on track toward attaining a particular goal" (p. 21). No longer can we maintain that conduct, whether private or public, is due only to environmental influences or genetic factors. In a self-regulation system choices are made on the basis of whether they match or contradict internal standards. These standards comprise conscience, determine the pattern of our daily lives, cause us to want to change the environment and the circumstances we face because of the behavior of others. As human beings we are capable of acting not only in a self-correcting way but in a manner that causes others to want to enhance their self-regulation ability.

Carver and Scheier believe this self-corrective system is composed of a hierarchy of constituents. At the top are the goals we set for ourselves followed by the principles we adhere to in attaining these goals, such as honesty and truthfulness. Below this level is our actual conduct, what we do in everyday life to attain our aspirations. Carver and Scheier stress that "one of the connotations of the term self-regulation is the sense of self-corrective adjustments being made as the person interacts with the world" (p. 158). Self-regulation means we conduct ourselves in a manner other than simply reacting. We are choosing, comparing, deciding, and drawing conclusions, not merely going along with whatever is happening. Moreover, self-regulation implies that what we do has meaning according to our internal standards. It is not drifting with the current. Our values are points of reference stored in memory. What confronts us evokes the value reference needed for making a response that does not contradict our standards of moral conduct. Carver and Scheier have shown that when people use internal controls, they adjust their expectations upward when they are successful and downward when they fail, to a greater extent than those who rely on external control. When moral values serve as a guide we adjust to the demands before us whereas, when someone else controls our conduct, we simply do what we are told. Some people are guided by socially determined judgments with deleterious consequences. They become victims of the whims or dictates of others, especially in the "gang culture." The implications for how we conduct ourselves and what we do to guide youth are great indeed.

Focusing on moral standards leads to more successful living personally and professionally. However, low self-esteem, anxiety, and depression disturb the ability to use self-regulation so our conduct becomes impulsive and demeaning or we do what we think will satisfy others. As individuals we want to satisfy our inner needs and be accepted by others. There is no substitute, however, for adhering to inner standards. It is easy for people, especially youth, to become overly responsive to "social control," thereby foregoing self-regulation. Self-monitoring must be ongoing. Those who are low on this ability act in random and poorly directed ways. Those who are high in self-monitoring exercise discretion and make choices based on the situation at hand. Their decisions reflect which circumstances are in conflict with or match internal standards. This process requires awareness of conflict. Self-regulation assumes self-evaluation, often not realized and fostered by society.

Poor self-monitoring is not an all or nothing process. We accept self-control to the extent that we will not commit murder (although many are unable to monitor themselves even at this level.) But we abuse others, cheat, steal, and engage in other immoral activity. We use self-evaluation in most situations but when angry or depressed we become destructive if not violent. If youth are not being given the moral training required for developing internal standards, they cannot avoid being irresponsible and blaming others for whatever occurs. There are variations in the extent to which each individual can be responsible for what happens, but a given level of morality is essential for us as individuals and as a society. Each one of us carries responsibility for our own conduct and for assisting others in gaining the self-control they need.

Internal Standards

Perhaps we should consider further what we mean by internal standards and how to use experience in making judgments. Carver and Scheier define a standard as a "standing behavioral pattern" (p. 122). Standards are used in many ways, in categorizing others, in being tolerant, intolerant, or blameful. We seek others to help us decide what our standards should be. We ask questions to substantiate the standards we are acquiring to learn more about how to react to others, to be aware of what is right and what is wrong. This seeking serves as a basis for growing up, for being able to assume responsibility. Unfortunately when youth seek such assistance, often it is unavailable because many parents have not established moral standards for themselves and are not in a position to guide their children, nor provide the instruction and example needed. Likewise, many agencies and institutions no longer have standards of morality to assist people in discriminating between good and evil. There is no question that the family is the primary source of such training and example. When families are not able to provide the necessary example everyone suffers. Under these circumstances children gain what conscience they can by observing others. Often the result is that the standards needed for moral living are not acquired. When conscience is absent, the worst should be expected. It leads to misguided, disturbed, and dangerous conduct. Only the conscience process gives us a basis for what we are doing and what we intend to do. Criminals are deficient in moral reasoning, being unable to fully realize the difference between moral and immoral behavior. Their ability to think in these terms is below average; they are unable to perceive differences in conduct that is clearly wrong or right. This is an important aspect of the psychology of criminality. The more we successfully evaluate ourselves, the better our judgment will be morally and spiritually. Moreover, this success leads to confidence and optimism. Carver and Scheier have shown that optimism leads to assurance in coping with life's stressfulness, prevents depression and feelings of helplessness.

An early analysis of the self-regulation process was made by Thoreson and Mahoney. They found that expectation of a favorable outcome is a significant factor in attaining successful self-control. Conscience is involved because it shows that values have been established. Behind this is the ability to forego immediate rewards for greater gains later. This is the covert, cognitive aspect of self-control. Tacit corruption leads to an inactive conscience. In their book Losing Control, Baumeister, Heatherton and Tice emphasize that conscience requires us to consider what lies beyond the immediate and what is beyond the actual situation before us. Preoccupation with immediate circumstances leads to self-regulation failure. We reject broader meanings and permit lower level meanings to take over. Self-regulation is most successful when long-term meanings are adhered to and processed by conscience. When conscience is weak and does not monitor adequately, broader meanings are overlooked. Effective monitoring and self-awareness assume continuous reflection about conduct, its implications for ourselves and for others, which raises the question of acquiescence. There are circumstances in which we give in to impulses. Self-regulation fails because circumstances are not under our control; it is not our fault. But if we give in to all manner of demands and do nothing about them, it is our fault; we are not being responsible.

With ineffective self-regulation we lay ourselves open to temptations, even being vulnerable to becoming criminals. Self-regulation consists of several factors, but the one which dominates is the ability to delay self-gratification. Control of gratification is so essential it warrants special understanding. The ability to defer immediate rewards, no matter how pleasant they may be, is crucial. Self-regulation assumes that internal standards have been established. If these standards are vague, poorly developed, confused, and weak, self-regulation cannot be achieved. Self-monitoring will be inadequate and failures such as those seen in crimes of obedience should be expected. Conscience must be equal to controlling impulses so conduct conforms to internalized values. In self-regulation one motive overrides others with the strength to control those that are unacceptable—the inclination to be untruthful, dishonest, or violent. Self-monitoring entails other aspects, such as having the internalized standards for making the required judgment; with lack of these standards self-control fails. A strong conscience provides motivation and determination to fulfill the demands of being in control. If our standards are not morally based with a focus on long-term goals, self-control will fail. What we believe about ourselves determines what we do. If we are afraid, we withdraw because of fear of failure. Weak people are unsuccessful in developing self-control and are victims of immoral influences. They cannot attain self-regulation without assistance and training. Without help they remain attached to immediate circumstances. Self-control entails long-range values, transcending the actual and being in control of one's destiny. It requires persistence. It is will-power in action. Self-awareness is part of this process. We must realize that we withdraw from activities which threaten our self-esteem. We may overestimate our abilities, leading to failure because of setting goals beyond our capabilities. People with low self-esteem set low goals with little meaning, whereas those with too high self-esteem try at all costs to prove they are right.

Ability to delay gratification is a fundamental aspect of self-control and leads to being competent, resourceful, and reasonable. When we are acquiescent we abandon disciplined effort for more immediate rewards. This is the opposite of long-range planning and leads to failure in self-control, a type of "self-handicapping" according to Baumeister, Heatherton, and Tice. We set up obstacles to performance because they serve our purposes. If we fail we can blame them; if we succeed we can boast about how good we are because we overcame them. Such self-handicapping reduces disgrace of failure and increases credit for success.

In addition to acquiescence, procrastination leads to self-destructive conduct which results from not setting realistic short-term goals. It may also be caused by setting too-high goals and then "giving up. " A significant aspect of procrastinating is withdrawing from what we should do because of anxiety; to engage in the activity might be overwhelming. Threats to our ego offer temptations to procrastinate. The feeling, "how will this reflect on me?" becomes predominant. Such reactions lead to failure in self-regulation. Success also presents problems because we follow only what led to it and do not see changes that need to be made to meet new demands. Success might lead to feeling that we do not need to try anymore.

Self-Deception

Disorders of self-perception are due to compulsions and obsessions which take many forms including drugs, sex, and violence. They may take the form of continuing to think about experiences despite efforts to stop doing so. Compulsions impede self-stopping because inhibitions are weak. Self-regulation fails because we cannot set limits. Inner control processes are inadequate. An overloaded mind is not free to consider relative choices; anxiety takes over and self-control suffers, sometimes seriously. Anything that overwhelms the system leads to the breakdown of self-regulation and normal operation of conscience. There are many obstacles to maintaining normal function including failure to try, weakness, not listening to its messages, trying to take shortcuts, and not holding ourselves responsible. These obstacles usually take the form of self-deception, in convincing ourselves of something we prefer to believe instead of accepting the facts as they are. We may begin by telling ourselves that our abilities are superior to others, we are better than our peers, when in fact this is not true. Recognizing this rationalization may be painful so we continue with the delusion to our detriment in handling what we face in daily life.

Often we are told we should not be concerned about self-regulation; we should express ourselves freely. This point of view is in error and leads to disruptive circumstances within families and society in general. To be told we must express all anger is intolerable and leads to vicious conduct. Venting is a breakdown in self-control. The argument that this is a way to prevent pent-up feelings is mistaken and leads to dangerous outcomes. Venting is ineffective in dealing with emotional turmoil. Giving in to our emotions, including anger, has the opposite effect because it causes feelings to become more out of control, reducing normal conscience function. Expressing anger leads to loss of self-regulation, not to gaining it. Ruminating about distraught feelings also leads to long-term distress. "Calming down" before encountering the issues involved enhances self-control. Giving in to temptation means we "comfort" ourselves by immediate gratification. Conscience demands self-awareness and causes us to compare actions with internal standards; it intervenes and stimulates self-regulation. Self-awareness, an off-shoot of conscience, reduces anxiety. Inhibition is the essence of self-awareness. Avoiding self-awareness leads to being unable to regulate oneself, which in turn is the basis for becoming involved in self-destructive activities. We must be aware that concentrating on immediate gratification leads to self-defeat whereas inhibitions and self-control enhance long-term goals and attainment of aspirations. Loss of control is a front runner in self-destructive behavior. Self-monitoring is an absolute necessity in maintaining self-control. A weak conscience is a fundamental deficiency in those who commit crimes. But other problems derive from this deficiency, such as eating disorders. At least one-third of Americans are more than fifteen percent overweight. Monitoring food intake is an example of self-regulation. How we perceive ourselves is an important aspect of self-awareness. Self-perception can be disturbed by fatigue, emotional distress, and other conditions.

Violence in the streets often leads to discussion of how law and order must be intensified. Although self-control is the main issue it is usually ignored. Virtually all aggression entails weakness in self-regulation. Criminality is a case in point. To engage in crime is to seek immediate gratification. Long-term goals and aspirations are overridden; that aggression begets aggression is ignored. An indulgent society urges us to forego long-term goals. Only when conscience alerts us to the short-term, self-indulgent nature of such urgings can we see that self-regulation is essential. We must guard against becoming acquiescent and keep long-term goals in mind. We have been led to believe that all feelings must be expressed. This is erroneous. Not all feelings can or should be expressed.

Self-Evaluation

Tesser says, "the self-evaluation model has at its core the assumption that persons behave so as to maintain a positive self-evaluation" (p. 204). We want to be assured we are doing well. We want a good self-image. We want to understand ourselves in relation to the world around us. In so doing we compare ourselves with others to check on our self-evaluation, noting whether it validates what we think of ourselves. Unless we have established internal standards we have no basis for making this comparison. Some of us see someone considered to be a "winner," and whatever this individual exemplifies is what we think is right. Companies recognize that this tendency to "follow the leader" is common so they exploit it to the fullest in their advertising. Threats to the opinions of ourselves are disturbing and must be handled properly. This too is part of the ability to evaluate ourselves. There are instances in everyone's life that indicate our self-evaluation is in error.

Self-Affirmation

Emphasis on self-esteem is often ill-advised. Kilpatrick points out that self-esteem is not simply a feeling to be taught in and of itself. He believes that "real self-esteem is a by-product of real learning and achievement. We feel good about ourselves because we have done something good or worthy" (p. 41). Self-esteem cannot be separated from what we do because it is rooted in how we show concern for our neighbors. In helping children gain self-esteem we must assist them to realize that this feeling is the result of worthy conduct.

We have learned the meaning of self-esteem mainly by studying those who have not attained it. Baumeister (1993) found that individuals with low self-esteem are deficient in the ability to describe their attributes and capabilities, are less stable and more cautious in personal relationships, and have a confused self-concept. Everyone at times feels that his or her self-image is threatened. Those with high self-esteem have the strength needed to cope with these threats, but those with low self-esteem struggle, become anxious and depressed. Many who help children gain self-esteem do not realize that conscience serves as the basis for self-affirmation. When what we do conforms with worthiness we gain feelings of self-worth, the foundation of self-esteem.

There are complexities in this aspect of conscience development which include feelings of self-enhancement and self-hatred. Those having low self-esteem follow a pattern of fear of failure because the more a given type of conduct is valued the more it is feared. If good grades in school or a high level of sales are highly valued they will be feared, meaning many daily expectations are threatening. Self-approval is a basic need and feeling that our conduct is worthy is part of our self-image which, together with the image of others, is essential to well-being emotionally and physically. Some resolve this need by identifying with those who feel good about themselves. Many with low self-esteem underestimate their strengths because their conscience is punitive. But emphasis on self-esteem causes some persons to become over-confident and unrealistic which also leads to failure. They do not realize that self-esteem cannot be taken on as a garment, that it must have a firm foundation in actuality. Without the attitude of doing what is worthy, conflicts are inevitable. Baumeister (1993) shows that those with low self-esteem sometimes conduct themselves in ways to convince others they are inadequate. In so doing they gain verification by causing others to see them as they see themselves. An understanding of conscience can assist those with low self-esteem to gain feelings of self-affirmation.

Low self-esteem and poor self-affirmation are related. Steele has contributed significantly to the knowledge of self-affirmation. He says we affirm ourselves according to the ways in which conscience is matched or violated. Hence, study of the psychology of self-affirmation is intertwined with the study of the psychology of self-regulation, which is related to "dissonance phenomenon," the feelings of conflict and stress that occur when we do not conform to our internal standards. When we do not adhere to what we expect of ourselves we feel dissonance. What is known as stress, referred to constantly in our society, is due not only to one's work-a-day world circumstances. It is caused by conflicts we feel when we cannot give ourselves the affirmation we need because our conduct is in conflict with what we expect of ourselves. This stressfulness may be seriously detrimental. It is unfortunate this dissonance phenomenon is not given the attention it warrants. It is a part of the conscience process everyone experiences. The function of conscience is highlighted by psychologists such as Steele who says, "the idea that cognitive inconsistency is disturbing and motivates consistency-restoring cognitive and behavioral changes is one of the founding ideas of contemporary social psychology" (p. 279). He emphasizes that stress and conflict result from violation of our internal standards and that this violation leads to our doing something about it. It is precisely in this way that conscience is crucial to conduct. Conscience is more than a system that alerts us to what we are doing. It also causes us to feel dissonance (often referred to as guilt), which causes us to change our conduct for the better. This is why we stress that we have a conscience because we need one. Integrity, the feeling that we have when we conform to our moral values, is a basic factor in conduct. Without a normally functioning conscience, integrity is not possible. Self-regulation, including self-affirmation, can be effective and creative only through the incorporation of moral values.

Jealousy and Envy

Although jealousy and envy are feelings that influence people every day, they have not been studied extensively, which is unfortunate because these feelings play a significant role in our lives. While jealousy and envy are similar, they can be differentiated. It is important to do so because many people suffer from disorders involving them. Both jealousy and envy can lead to loss of self-control and violence. A common occurrence is the way these feelings disrupt families. Our emphasis is on the role of conscience in maintaining self-control when jealousy and envy become predominant and personal relationships deteriorate. First we differentiate these feelings.

Envy is a feeling that occurs when we desire something another person has. It occurs mainly when we think the abilities and achievements of others reflect on us, causing feelings of inferiority or ill-will. The core of envy is social comparison, primarily with peers. It breaks in when our self-concept is threatened. In contrast to emulation, envy motivates us to take steps to hinder someone so he cannot have what we desire. We feel others are causing us to lack what we want. This causes frustration, makes us aware of our inferiorities, and leads to anxiety.

Jealousy is the feeling we have when we fear losing an important relationship to a rival. It always entails loss to a competitor. Behind this feeling is an urgent desire to be needed. Envy occurs when someone has something we desire. Jealousy is a feeling of loss of a relationship. Someone's gain is our loss; the common thread is suspicion together with anger. In envy we make a social comparison, but in jealousy we compare ourselves with the individual of whom we are jealous. Envy often includes feelings of injustice and hostility whereas jealousy is a protective reaction covering attempts to cope. Jealousy occurs when we have a commitment and feel this commitment is failing. This feeling of failure leads to other threats such as insecurity and anxiety. These feelings raise our level of arousal so we are further threatened, especially by our self-concept. Jealousy is a fundamental way in which we show our need to be liked and accepted. We want to maintain a relationship because it is perceived as a means whereby we can maintain self-esteem. The two most common causes of jealousy are threats to self-esteem and threats to relationships. It is a complex feeling that may include anger, fear, sadness, sexual arousal, and guilt. It also entails possessiveness because the individual involved is expected to conform to our wishes, not to the wishes of others. These feelings are vulnerable to a breakdown of self-control which can lead to violence.

White and Mullen say, "ordinary and otherwise unremarkable individuals in the grips of jealousy may be prey to experience that at other times they would consider totally alien to their normal character" (p. 174). Most of us are unaware we are jealous or envious. Salovey emphasizes that jealousy "occurs when the superior qualities, achievements, or possessions of another are perceived as reflecting badly on the self" (p. 4). We feel jealous when we are disposed to feel inferior or resentful. Although jealousy at times may be normal often it results in loss of self-control. Conscience is involved because jealousy entails internalized feelings of who we are. Self-evaluation is threatened. Control of jealousy and envy is dependent on a normally functioning conscience.

Rationalization

Most of us want to be rational and use good judgment. But sometimes rationalization is used to avoid responsibility or to avoid taking a position on issues of immorality. We "talk" to ourselves to explain what we have done. Rationalization is common in daily life. We see someone being victimized but do nothing to help, rationalizing that its not my affair, I should not get involved, its not my problem. These rationalizations go on every day—we bribe our conscience. Our conscience warns us that what we are observing is wrong. We experience dissonance, feel conflict, and the need to relieve these feelings. What shall I do? It is easy to regain a feeling of not being in conflict by saying it is not my problem. Sometimes this is all we need to relieve our feelings. But we must realize that more than ever in our history such apathy is one of the greatest evils we face. To accept responsibility for moral conduct is vital to changing the pattern of violence in communities and neighborhoods. Apathy, the result of rationalization, is not acceptable. Moral principles are avoided through rationalization. The judgments required cannot be made in a moral vacuum. Rationalization as a way of life is dangerous. It results in superficial, inappropriate, shallow conclusions, rather than responsible, moral conduct. As Williams (1989) states, "seemings, and acceptance of seemings, instead of true morality, true courage, true character: that is a most painful demand" (p. 6). He continues, "the development of character and values, as opposed to the mere putting on of what seems to be moral, must begin with the realization that such rational, speculative, purely academic means are worse than not enough" (p. 7). We have a values gap between rationalization and responsible moral behavior. We cannot have a free society by pursuing wealth alone. Materialistic preoccupations lead to increasing secularization, not to the moral values crucial to every person on earth.

Wiggins in a discussion of needs, values, and truth comments, "it is a terrible thing to try to live a life without believing in anything" (p. 89). Sometimes it seems this is what we are trying to do. Nickerson observes, "as a parent and grandparent, I am concerned about some current trends and would like to understand better what can be done to increase the probability that the world we are bequeathing to future generations is one they will want to inhabit" (p. ix). These authorities highlight the significance of internal standards. This is true also of the observations by Meninger. More than two decades ago this great psychiatrist wrote, "in various cubbyholes of my mind are variations and elaborations, but basic distinctions of my mother and father remain my conscience code book." He emphasized that we no longer consider anything wrong. We are no longer "sinners." It is the fault of someone else: parents, minorities, clergymen. We relieve our conscience by attributing immoral conduct to "illnesses," often called addictions. Addictions have become excuses for self-indulgence and for not being responsible for what we do. This too is a form of rationalization. We seek power to gain affluence and what we assume will bring self-esteem. But what we are doing is following the path of expediency; standards of value become secondary. When asked about our motives we make claims of being moral. In many instances this is a superficial rationalization. It is only when values become primary that we can assume responsibility for moral conduct.

It is common to refer to high-risk behavior as addictive, placing responsibility for that behavior on the addiction instead of on the person. For example, alcoholism is viewed as a disease so the individual is excused for being an alcoholic; the same can be said for a variety of conduct disorders, such as overeating and dependency on drugs. Without denigrating efforts to help persons with such problems, we raise the question of whether this assistance causes some to become dependent, if not irresponsible. Peele and Brodsky say, "the disease model of addiction does more harm than good because it does not give people enough credit for their resilience and capacity to change" (p. 13). They continue, "it fails to hold them accountable for acting irresponsibly while under the influence of alcohol or drugs, or for excessive behavior ranging from shopping to gambling" (p. 14). These authorities respect every person's ability to make good choices, even those who have severe compulsive disorders. They refuse to undermine the individual's integrity, giving everyone credit for being capable of self-control. To say one's conduct is not under his control because of heredity or illness is arbitrary, untrue, and without benefit because it prevents us from making necessary decisions and taking action. It is a framework for failure and suggests that the health-behavior problem is life-long, although usually it is not. Addictions are the outcome of choices which have led to a pattern of losing self-control. Attempts to overcome addictions without considering the moral-health implications usually are not successful. Peele and Brodsky point out, "we must not apologize for asking people to behave well or for teaching and expecting children to contribute to the well-being of others" (p. 375).

Other patterns of rationalization in our culture interfere with conscience development. We bestow rewards and prizes for almost anything, important or trivial. Children are given rewards for a variety of reasons, but usually because we want them to conform in some way. This results in their doing what is considered right for extraneous reasons. Rewards used in this way stifle the desire to achieve for moral considerations. The prize becomes the primary motivation when actual achievement is the primary value and the basis for developing character. In conscience development it is what the child does for himself and for others that provides feelings of satisfaction. We cannot over-emphasize the importance of this principle when helping children learn what it means to do what is right versus what is wrong. It is not uncommon to see rewards become deadening and defeat the development of values and the satisfaction of feeling genuine achievement when one does his best for important reasons. Teenagers often do better when they are not given rewards, but given direction in ways they can help others. Motivation, why we do what we do, is crucial to conduct. In most people there is a desire to attain self-control because loss of it leads to disasters, large or small. When given the necessary guidance and training we enjoy demonstrating our capacity for self-regulation.

There are other considerations in using rewards to control behavior. Using rewards is based on the assumption that human beings should be trained and controlled in the same way as lower animals. This fallacious assumption has been used in some schools of thought for decades if not centuries. It is time we recognize that this mechanistic approach overlooks the fact that human beings are different from lower animals. Not the least of these differences is the fact that human beings develop a conscience, learn self-control, have spiritual needs and feelings, and a desire to be of service to others. It is strange yet not uncommon that we over-simplify who we are, not realizing why we resent being treated in the simplistic, mechanistic way portrayed in advertising; the approach which says that if you will follow these simple steps your reward will be a life of joy forever. Simplistic rewards do not help children understand principles such as "we should not do that which is harmful to ourselves or others" and that life not only is endurable but joyful and meaningful. It is in this sense that rewards often detract and impede conscience development.

Hope

Consideration of conscience cannot overlook hope because conscience and hope are related. We are hopeful when we are successful in conducting ourselves in harmony with internalized moral standards. It is difficult to feel hopeful if we are in conflict with what we believe to be right. Only when we are at peace can we be hopeful for ourselves and for others. There are persons who view hope as being detrimental and unrealistic. Hope is the basis of well-being, the process of seeing what can and should be done for the betterment of ourselves and people everywhere. Snyder says, "hope is the sum of the mental willpower and waypower that you have for your goals" (p. 5). Hope involves aspirations that have a possibility of being attained, not aspirations for which there is no possibility.

We all seek meaningfulness and there is no more important role for us as adults than to be meaning-makers. There is much poverty around the world, but there is another urgent problem not due to lack of material wealth. This is the spiritual poverty caused by lack of moral values. Money is not a substitute for moral standards that motivate people to use self-control and to serve others. We no longer view work as a mission. It is what is done to earn a livelihood. The truly poor are those who lack vital purpose in life. It is these persons who face hopelessness. Meyers defines feelings of well-being as "a pervasive sense that life is good" (p. 23). Greater material success has not brought these feelings. In fact material advantage has helped us to realize we are starving spiritually.

Will power and hope are not equivalent. Will power is determination to attain hope, our determination to overcome difficulties and the process whereby we attach ourselves to potential success. Those who are hopeful, in comparison with those who are cynical, are not hostile; they have a sense of humor and are more satisfied with themselves. It is not the same as intelligence. Many individuals with high intelligence fail to develop hopefulness. It is a way of thinking about ourselves in relation to our capabilities.

Persons having high hopes do better in all phases of living; they have less burnout, more and better goals, anticipate the future, and have greater happiness. They interact easily with others and take more chances. Hope and optimism are related; hope correlates with feelings of being in control, of having charge of one's destiny. Those who have high hopes are not dependent on others for maintaining self-control because they have a strong sense of self-direction. Moreover, they have high capabilities in problem solving. They are not necessarily out to win but in a cooperative way they are competitive. They are concerned about the process of living and have high levels of self-esteem. Hope is closely associated with high energy because of its integration with positive feelings—hopelessness is fatiguing. High-hope people choose more complex goals and maintain better health. High-hope teenagers have fewer behavior problems and enter adulthood more successfully. Those having high hope control work-stress more easily and focus attention on solving problems, whereas low-hope people are characterized by an inability to form relationships. As high-hope people become elderly they show satisfaction with their lives and are not regretful or pessimistic. Hopeful people do not fear death; hopefulness remains stable.

Development of Hope

We are not born hopeful. There is close association between hope and conscience; one cannot be considered without the other inasmuch as hopefulness is an aspect of a well-developed conscience. It is associated with trust and trustworthiness, a basic feeling in emotional development. Hope develops as the child begins to trust others. We have indicated how this feeling is related to identification with parents in early life. It is important to remember that trust is learned. Hopefulness develops largely from successful interaction with others. It is helpful when parents teach children words that signify hope because development of language and hope are associated. But there is no alternative to having successful experiences, no matter how trivial. Hope and achievement are related. Hope is future oriented so anticipation of the future is part of hope. Children who have supportive parents who teach them how to overcome obstacles and give them opportunities for making decisions and relying on internal controls are higher in feelings of hope and show less depression. The emotional basis for hope appears during the first two years of life. Having no hope is one of the greatest handicaps anyone can encounter. It colors every aspect of living and frequently is the cause of depression, abusiveness, alcoholism, drug addiction, or criminal behavior. Hopelessness may be one of the most intense influences in gang activities and street violence.

There are reasons for feeling hopeless, bearing in mind that hope is learned. It must be developed through training in the home—hopeful parents have hopeful children. Anger and rage must be recognized as feelings that destroy hope. Anger results in feelings of despair and cynicism. These feelings tell us we no longer expect to achieve so we give in to apathy. Loss of hope is the primary cause of depression. Because of inadequate parenting some children never receive the support needed for the development of hope. Other children receive support in early life, but because of circumstances encountered later they lose it and suffer neglect. Many adults report that they did not receive support during childhood. This seems to account for about half of the hopelessness felt during adult life. We hear much about children who are abused, but neglected children suffer a greater breakdown emotionally. Neglected and abused children do not learn hopefulness. All children must feel attachment for hope to develop. The death of a parent or a divorce often causes difficulties in attaining hope. Anything that obliterates the attachment process can cause disturbances in learning to be hopeful; family dysfunctions are devastating.

Low-hope persons feel more lonely and are less able to confide. They feel "unconnected," a severe handicap in the development of conscience. Burnout is a factor because it reflects hope being extinguished. When we feel loss of hope we seek excuses for it. For example the tendency to excuse drug addiction, alcoholism, or sexual abuse as *conditions* for which we are not responsible. This feeling is not helpful because it does not provide the hope we need to manage our behavior successfully. Other factors that cause hopelessness include racial prejudice, discrimination, poverty, and lack of moral values. Under these circumstances people reduce their goals and hopes. Not being able to freely pursue important goals results in feeling hopeless. These are significant factors because the lack of goals and friends leads to suicidal thinking and depression even more than the use of drugs. High-hope people have other advantages. They shift goals if a goal becomes unattainable whereas low hope people continue to pursue goals that are out of reach. High-hope people set their own goals—they are not followers. They are creative when dealing with obstacles, realizing that one must learn to be patient, adept in delaying gratification, and able to enjoy the process, not only the end results. They have few "down-times." Unlike low-hope individuals they find few faults in themselves and do not reflect deficiencies.

Hope is an attitude of concern. It colors and influences interpersonal relationships. It is a way in which we can better understand others. Hopeful, cheerful teenagers become fulfilled, happy adults. Feelings of confidence and self-control are predictive of well-being. Hope reflects optimism, not despair, and optimists are healthier and enjoy greater success. We help others when we show them they are capable of giving love. Hope is an outstanding aspect of conscience. It is one of the greatest gifts that life affords. It means we view life with an eternal perspective that relieves fear and apprehension. It permits us to delight in the gifts of each day.

Hutschnecker states it well when he says that hope sustains life and hopelessness causes death. Hope is the uplifting power that creates momentum and alerts us to action. It overcomes obstacles and serves as a source of inspiration. Hope is essential for joyful living. It is the source of optimism, the attitude that counteracts depression and tells us that all will turn out well. It is the opposite of morbidity, which leads to preoccupation with death. A creative, wholesome life is dependent on hopefulness. Hopelessness leads to self-hate. It is the role of conscience to integrate feelings and provide self-control so that hope can prevail. Hope provides spiritual power to overcome cynicism by alerting us to withstand impulses leading to immorality. Conscience serves as the basis for hope, for expectation of goal attainment.

Hopefulness is necessary for planned action. One's level of hope develops from success and failure, experiences monitored by conscience. If hope is unrealistic conscience alerts us to the need for modification of our aspirations. It is hopefulness which is the foundation of a desire to achieve. Hopefulness generates similar feelings in others. It serves as the basis of spirituality because, although hopefulness and spirituality are not identical, one leads to the other.

CHAPTER IV

Conscience Disorders

If conscience does not develop, the implications are frightening for us as individuals and for society. It may develop and provide awareness of right and wrong or it may become "an immoral conscience" (Eigen). Having a conscience means we experience feelings of guilt, shame, and remorse. These are normal feelings and form the complex of a working conscience. Sometimes these feelings are excessive and dominate us, manifesting a conscience disorder and a need for psychotherapeutic assistance.

Those who lack feelings of remorse are designated as psychopaths. Some individuals do not lack a conscience but have one that is disordered, being so punitive that they relinquish all feelings of right and wrong. Eigen says an immoral conscience sometimes is caused by feelings of self-righteousness. His view is "that psychopaths lack a conscience is wrong. The problem is they have too much of the wrong kind of conscience. A voice tells them that they are right to steal, kill, maim, injure, whatever their heart desires; it is only just" (p. 33). He goes on to explain that an immoral conscience ignores past experience. An example is a rapist who said he thought of an immoral conscience as a feeling that "everything is OK unless it hurts me." Another example is a 16-year-old male youth who had stolen a car. He was being held at a detention home and his parents asked that he be given leave to go home for Thanksgiving. Against professional advice the judge gave permission for him to do so. He had sufficient funds to take a bus but instead surveyed the streets nearby, found a car with keys in it, jumped in and drove it to his home. As Eigen emphasizes these persons seem to feel justified in doing anything they desire but have no awareness of the consequences. A normally functioning conscience would alert them to what they have done and cause them to face the circumstances. Eigen summarizes by stating, "Human-

Conscience Disorders

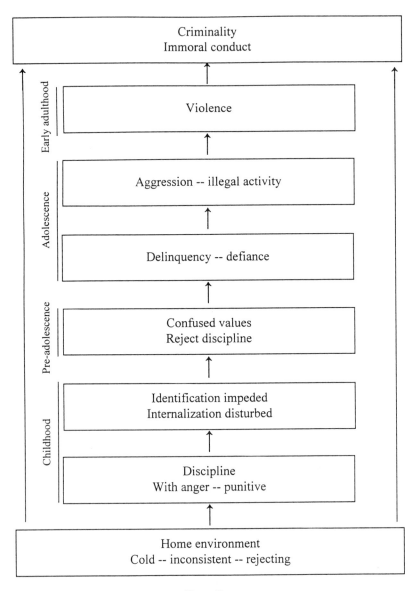

kind is now at a place where the work of immoral conscience is poisoning the planet and the goodness of law is made poisonous or vacuous by cynical manipulation, disregard, or fundamentalist rigidity" (p. 16).

Conscience disorders do not develop suddenly. They are acquired over time. Sometimes these disorders are severe, as in those whom we have referred to as being conscienceless. Individuals who are fully grown physically and intellectually but who are without self-control are to be feared. The development of conscience disorders is shown schematically in Figure Two. Not all conscience disorders begin in early childhood, but many do and often it is these that result in violent conduct. On the other hand, early childhood experience might be adequate, but because the family pattern changes with poor supervision and dysfunctional patterns operating, conscience development can be impeded at the preadolescent or adolescent period. If conscience disorders are to be prevented consistent discipline must be provided from childhood into adulthood.

The emotional climate of the home and the attitudes and methods used in discipline provide the foundation for conscience development. Consistency is vital because it shows how right and wrong differ, that moral values are stable and do not vary from one situation to another. Arousal level is another factor of importance. As discussed previously, arousal level is the point at which we become sensitive to messages from conscience. If we ignore these inner signals we cannot be sensitive to our feelings nor to the feelings of others. We know that unless children and youth are made aware of right and wrong, consistently and patiently, they do not acquire the ability to perceive evil for what it is. They see conduct which obviously is wrong, sometimes even dangerous, but do not identify it as such, a common finding in the study of delinquents. Their arousal level is low, so they do not normally identify wrong conduct as being wrong. This pattern has been observed in adult criminals as well. Deficits in arousal level are one of the most fundamental aspects of the psychology of criminality and one of the primary characteristics of those who have conscience disorders. Rapists and pedophiles, for example, often do not view themselves as offenders; they say that what they do is not victimizing. Their arousal level is flagrantly defective so they have no shame or remorse. Not all conscience disorders are discernible but many of them are. Diagnosticians are called upon to recognize them, not to overlook their potential for causing violence.

The study of conscience disorders is in its infancy, but it promises to provide a basis for identifying conduct which not only is demeaning but threatening and dangerous. The schema shown in Figure Two is not intended as an inclusive depiction of the development of these disorders but as a framework for further study and for emphasizing the developmental aspects. Certain types of violence, such as wife-abuse, might fall at the disturbed-arousal level because the husband is unaware of the evil involved in what he is doing. Many immoral acts, especially in preadolescence, fall at the level of confusion about what is right and what is wrong; their insight regarding feelings and motives falls below average. Fortunately, studies are beginning to show that proper training in self-understanding is effective. When children and adults are given guidance and instruction in morally understanding the differences between right and wrong they gain self-control. We must not permit cynicism to dominate decisions in developing ways to assist those who are vulnerable to criminality.

How can parents help their child develop a good conscience? As shown in Figure Two the pattern of child management that damages conscience development has been determined. The emotional climate of the home not only is the first consideration, but it is the most important. If parental attitudes are cold, rejecting, and punitive, children are unable to form emotional attachment; they cannot achieve bonding, the most crucial aspect of emotional development. Disruption at this level is one of the most damaging children encounter. Neglect, in the sense of inadequate attention and emotional security, is extremely damaging emotionally, even more than physical punishment. Disruption of emotional development disturbs identification so moral values cannot be internalized, leading to defiance, aggression, and violence. Conscience development can be achieved only when parents are not punitive; *firmness without anger* is an effective principle to follow.

As shown in Figures One and Two there are ways in which conscience development can be fostered. But we must first recognize the significance of this self-control process and give it the attention required. A disordered, inadequate conscience is a vicious lifelong handicap. Unless the stages outlined in Figure One are recognized and proper guidance provided, there may be serious consequences as outlined in Figure Two.

Children who have disturbed relationships with parents at an early age suffer the most severe handicaps (see the first two levels in Figure Two). When discipline consists of anger and punitiveness, identification is impeded and standards for right and wrong cannot be internalized, preventing conscience development. The child becomes confused about values, leading to defiance and delinquency.

Anger

There are types and degrees of conscience disorders. We have mentioned the major problem of being conscienceless. A more pervasive disorder is the loss of conscience that prevails during temper outbursts, while feeling depressed, or undergoing attacks of anxiety. When anger is in control conscience is submerged and violent attacks occur. Likewise when depression or anxiety take over we are unable to follow what is right. We think only about our situation, not realizing that what we are doing is self-defeating. When these feelings overtake us, we are unable to respond to conscience so it is not always a predictor of what we will do. We should not find fault with how conscience functions, however. It is not a system that withstands all outbreaks. After a temper outburst there are feelings of remorse, even pleas for forgiveness because our conscience is aware of the outbreak and is alerting us to the fact that temper outbursts and violence are wrong. No one follows his conscience perfectly, but when a mature conscience has been attained it is a significant factor in helping to control outbursts. A fully developed conscience is the best control system we have. It warns us of consequences before we engage in hostile acts.

Shame

We become aware of conscience in various ways. Mead says, "shame, the agony of being found wanting and exposed to the disapproval of others, becomes a more prominent sanction behind conduct than guilt, the fear of measuring up to the high standards which are represented by the parents" (p. 660). Ausobel empha-

sizes another aspect when he defines conscience as a feeling of
obligation to abide by internalized moral values. He concludes:

> guilt is one of the most important psychological mechanisms
> through which an individual becomes socialized in the ways of
> his culture, and a social order unbuttressed by a sense   o f
> moral obligation in its members would enjoy precious little sta-
> bility. (p. 183)

Feelings of guilt are behind many outbreaks of discord and conflict. Nelson (1973) says these feelings focus "on powerful inner
urgings that warn, haunt, threaten, cajole, or lure whenever we are
facing alternate ways of acting" (p. 3). Sometimes there is a strong
subjective pressure, as though we are being overwhelmed by a
crushing burden. We feel we are facing an invisible jury determining the extent of our transgressions, telling us what is wrong and
inflicting suffering. Guilt is one of the most powerful emotions
affecting peace of mind.

Assagioli helps us understand these experiences. He says that
through technology we have much control over nature but the
basis for control of our inner being has been neglected. The gap
between external and inner power must be recognized. Inner
strength must control the outer. To become victimized by external
achievements is to be in danger of extermination. Conscience is
the process whereby the inner and outer worlds are integrated.
This integration causes us to be aware of our humanity and shows
us what it means to love others. Katz reminds us that conscience
includes awakening us to the broad problem of evil, which he says
is "behavior that deliberately deprives innocent people of their
humanity, from small scale assaults on a person's dignity to out-
right murder" (p. 5).

Shame and guilt can be differentiated. Nathanson says, "shame
is a universal experience" (p. 3). Shame, like guilt, is part of the
conscience process and not always detrimental. Everyone, no matter what level of education or occupation, will have feelings that
would be damaging if acted upon. Moreover, the actions of other
people might cause us to feel ashamed. These feelings are telling
us that conscience is working. When shame is extreme, the result
is shyness, undue modesty, embarrassment, feelings of ridicule,
and humiliation. The question is whether our feelings of shame

impede judgment and relationships. Wurmser stresses that shame occurs when we fear being disgraced, causing anxiety about our being looked upon with contempt because of something we have done. Shame follows being exposed when our conduct reflects badly on us. Our actions reveal we did not do what was expected of us. Wurmser says, "we are standing under the glare of one's own mind's eye" (p. 67).

Wurmser stresses that shame and guilt stand guard over both external and internal life, but he distinguishes between these feelings. He says, "shame refers to some sort of failure, weakness or flaw of the self, while guilt refers to some violation or attack upon the other" (p. 87). Parents frequently use shame as a way of controlling their children. In fact, many of us use this approach in dealing with others in the family, in the work place, and with friends. A statement such as "surely you know better than that" carries an underlying meaning that the person should be ashamed. Shamefulness often can be observed by others causing more humiliation, whereas guilt feelings are not observable. Shame is felt in the presence of those who are close to us. Guilt is more personal and does not necessarily involve others.

Feeling blameful is not necessarily wrong. Solnit studied youth and young adults and found that self-blame often leads to corrective action. He discusses "social conscience," which he defines as the individual's ability to feel self-approval or disapproval as he participates in social groups. Social support which requires moral conduct is a fundamental aspect of a free society. Our inclination is to view gang behavior punitively, as a law-and-order problem, but conscience is a crucial factor. Many boys engage in disruptive behavior because of a need for self-approval, particularly before ten years of age. Unfortunately, unless the meaning of this disorder is recognized, it remains into adulthood with criminal overtones.

The work of Nathanson provides additional insight on conscience disorders. He states there is "new attention to such matters as shyness, modesty, embarrassment, ridicule, and humiliation, . . . so our theoretical structures must be altered" (p. 1). He explains that much of what we know about conscience has derived from work with abnormal persons; now the normal must be heard from. We need to become more aware of the role of conscience in our lives. Nathanson's analysis makes this clear. He states that shame is a universal experience which brings on feelings of isolation. He observes, "to our list of words implying acute lowering of self-esteem we may add shyness, bashfulness, and modesty, as well as the experiences of being put-down, slighted, and thought of as contemptible. Disgrace, dishonor, degradation, and debasement involve closely related states" (p. 3). Shame follows exposure when others become aware of what we have done. On the other hand, guilt is a private matter and does not include the feelings or judgment of others.

Anger sometimes overrides conscience. Anger and shamefulness are related because anger serves to obscure feelings of shame. In our innermost feelings we tolerate outbursts of anger more successfully than feelings of shame. Some individuals who suffer depression feel shame-loaded. Usually it is necessary to explain to them that a conscience disorder underlies this emotional disturbance. "Shameless" people suffer from arrested conscience development. Shame follows being exposed, as having acted in a way that reflects badly on us. It follows the realization that we have not lived up to what our conscience tells us we should have done. Because shame suggests failure, weakness, or flaw, these feelings are difficult to tolerate. Shame causes us to feel inferior. Most adults regard shame as being childish and inappropriate. Shame can be used to control others, especially children, because we threaten them by what we say or do, indicating that we are going to make them feel shameful. Causing others to feel shameful is a way of humiliating them, a common pattern in everyday life.

The study of shame in relation to conscience has progressed rapidly in recent years, as shown by the work of Nichols. He points out that shamefulness may lead to insecurity and lack of self-respect. He says, "self-respect is the feeling of being whole, worthwhile and valued from within" (p. 16). Only a mature conscience can lead to feelings of wholeness, to awareness of how feelings of shame tell us that what we have done or are contemplating is wrong. This is the normal role of such feelings and should not be eliminated. When feelings of shame and remorse become overwhelming we should be aware that there is a disorder of conscience. It is not uncommon to find that individuals having this disorder are defiant and provocative. When confronted they become obstructive and try to control the threat of being humiliated. As Nichols observes, "shameless means acting without restraint and doing so brazenly" (p. 67). Underneath shame is embarrassment which leads to insecurity, fear, anxiety, and loss of self-esteem. When shame becomes disturbing there are ways in which it can be modified. We must face up to it, recognize our need for acceptance, and refuse to give in to the avoidance of others. We must accept who we are and not react only to what we have done. We must realize that self-control operates in a circle; one's relationship with oneself affects relationships with others. The more others accept us the more we gain self-assurance and self-respect. Those who attain a wholesome conscience understand what shame means.

Social Perception

Our study of prisoners shows the importance of conscience. A poorly developed conscience is a tragic handicap which leads to criminality and corruption. One of the ways in which this can be demonstrated is in what we have designated as social perception, the ability to perceive the meaning of what others do. It is a non-verbal process we use when surveying our environment as being safe or threatening. Children must learn what their social circumstances are and behave accordingly, which is a complex and intricate process. Only in recent years have we realized that some children have difficulty in doing this; they are classified as having a nonverbal learning disability. There are, however, children who do not achieve the expected level of social perception for other reasons, mainly because of neglect or abuse. When this occurs internalization of values is difficult. Conscience development is impeded, leaving them vulnerable to criminality. There is a connection between conscience and social perception. When conscience is disordered or poorly developed we can assume social perception will be impaired. We emphasize the importance of evaluating this ability when considering those disposed to criminality; without this consideration they cannot be adequately understood. Many criminals have social-perception disorders.

A disorder of social perception may be due to lack of training as seen in the effects of a dysfunctional family. It is in the family that children first learn the meaning of what others do, what kindness means, what being threatened means, the basics of social perception. These aspects of daily conduct need emphasis because they reflect conscience development. The entire family structure—parents, brothers, sisters, uncles, aunts, and others—is involved in conscience development. If family attitudes are suspicion, anxiety, hostility, depression, and defensiveness, conscience development is impeded if not precluded. Children must learn that violence is destructive, that anger begets anger, and that hatred is self-defeating.

Neglect in the study of social perception is shown by the way in which we glamorize violence. We know that children who view violence on television are more disposed to violent conduct. If we tolerate, in fact make a business of, violence, we should not be surprised that children and youth view such conduct as normal. A first step in controlling violence is to stop glamorizing it on television and elsewhere. When we profess that violence is wrong but make it an industry we cannot expect it to be controlled.

What should we do? First we can be positive. An optimistic approach is far more effective than simply emphasizing the negative. There is much for us to feel grateful about. We should not be indifferent. Behind all efforts must be the values we cherish: honesty, integrity, kindness, respect, and love for each other.

Restraint

Conscience restrains us from committing violence. The prevalence of violence at all levels of society indicates that conscience is not being developed adequately. Morality is often overlooked because of the emphasis on secularization. Spirituality and the sacredness of life are rarely mentioned. As meaning-makers, it is our responsibility to counter this neglect and point out that omission of spiritual values leads to loss of moral standards.

There are many ways in which to show how conscience is instrumental in restraining violence. Toch's study of men who committed violent crimes is an illustration. He found that they differ from the normal. Some became violent because they thought their reputation had been smeared and they felt humiliated. These men had intense needs for love and acceptance and, as a result, derogatory remarks caused them to lose control and commit violent acts. Their need to protect their feelings took command and overcame their capacity for self-control. Others in the study had low self-esteem, felt unworthy as though they had nothing to lose, and were not deserving. Their conscience being weak, self-control could not be activated. Another group was characterized by a need to fulfill a role perceived as being right for them. This role, unfortunately, involved displaying who they were regardless of its effect on others. To fulfill this role became an obligation. Although not articulated by Toch, there are criminals who suffer from conscience disorders in all of these groups. They are egocentric, self-indulgent, and their welfare is their only concern. They expect those around them, family and friends, to be responsive to their egocentric needs. When this does not happen they believe they are free to commit violence, revealing their conscience disorder. They feel they have been diminished and their reaction is to engage in violence.

A major concern is the question of why loss of control occurs. An important factor is age. Children who show aggression in the first ten years of life are likely to continue to be aggressive, hostile, and destructive. Parents may not realize that aggressive children often become destructive and turn to criminality in adolescence or early adulthood. Preventive programs need to be initiated immediately when vindictive, assaultive trends are observed. Unfortunately, the belief that these trends will be outgrown is still common, but this assumption is false. Preventive action must be undertaken.

Our era is not highly sensitive to the pervasive violence in society. Violence is one of the most profitable pursuits of all commercial enterprises. A great deal of money is made by selling violence. Until we recognize that this enterprise is causing serious harm we will not develop programs to stop it. Ours is a culture where violence for violence's sake is the norm, not the exception. Behind conscience training is the underlying message that violence is wrong and development of self-control is imperative for the well-being of all. It is not to our credit that we are the most violent in comparison with people in other nations. We need to gain control of the forces behind these circumstances. This means we must become more cognizant of the fundamental role of conscience. Children must be given moral training if they are to have the self-control necessary to refrain from violence. This is the basis for reducing criminality and random violence in homes and elsewhere. There is no alternative to recognizing the role of hostility. Perhaps all violence is not due to losing control; however, there is no question that the ultimate factor in self-control is being able to control anger. Outbursts of temper are behind most violent acts. To over-look the relationship between anger and violence is naive. No pro-gram for the development of self-discipline can be successful without awareness of this relationship.

However, we are confronted with a type of violence that may be new in our era. We are referring to the phenomenon of violence without anger. Due to the alienation incumbent in a secularized society, we are capable of depersonalizing experience in a way that results in violence without being angry, which characterizes van-dalism and some types of murder. This behavior illustrates a severe conscience disorder, even to the extent that the person committing the violence does not think of it as being wrong. Obviously this portrays a socio-cultural climate which is related to the way we conduct ourselves. We make it easy for individuals with con-science disorders to engage in violence. Instead of glamorizing vio-lence, we need to understand it for what it is, the conduct of persons who either have lost control or have not gained it. As a nation we need to recognize that individuals who lose control are dangerous and in need of psychological assistance, including con-science development. It is conscience that reveals the level of self-control of which each of us is capable.

The Cycle of Violence

Two common types of violence against children are abuse and neglect. Attention to these forms of violence is urgent because both are severely damaging. Referred to as the *cycle of violence*, abuse and neglect predispose children to crime. It is imperative that parents and professionals recognize that children who are neglected are likely to become violent offenders as they grow into adolescence and adulthood. We cannot assume that because child-ren are not physically abused they are cared for adequately. It is not only violent treatment that leads to violent behavior. Neglect is even more devastating according to Widow. Abandonment in the form of neglect is damaging and leads to violence. We should not find this surprising because we know attachment to parents is essential in emotional development. Neglect prevents bonding. If we are to develop programs of prevention we need to consider parental neglect as well as abuse. LeBlanc studied family inter-relationships and found marital conflicts weaken bonds between parents and their children and predispose them to adult criminality.

Gradually we are becoming able to predict which children will become violent. Aggression at eight years of age is a predictor of aggression at nineteen years of age irrespective of IQ, social class, or parents' level of aggressiveness. Watching TV increases disruptive behavior and leads to violence. Identification with parents lowers aggression. Those who engage in aggression have witnessed it or have been a part of it previously. If we are to reduce violence we need a broad change in the values that we proclaim. We cannot continue to saturate childrens' lives with violence and weapons.

Not all violence is overt. There is also passive violence. This is what is meant by neglect. Much of what is done to hurt others is not outwardly observable. We permit or engage in violence when we know abuse is occurring but do nothing to prevent it, for example, ignoring vandalism. If we took such violence seriously it could be greatly reduced if not eliminated. One of the ways in which violence occurs is at random, without purpose or meaning, especially in the form of drive-by shootings. Some youth state openly that their criminality is for excitement.

There is a need for a moral awakening. Our approach is to educate for power, not for compassion. The result is that people are seeking spiritual values to inspire them in their personal and professional lives. The complexity of technological living presents a special need for meaning and ways to resolve daily problems. Some doubt our ability to deal with the moral choices before us. They wonder about the integrity of our leaders and are alarmed about widespread moral decay. We need new perspectives, moral courage, and spiritual concepts for our personal lives and for society in general. This is precisely the role of values, standards which serve as guides for daily living.

Childhood aggression must be seen as a form of developmental psychopathology and treated in a timely manner. To delay treatment is to encourage criminal behavior at a later age. A more general perspective, however, is essential if such treatment is to be most effective. We must be aware that conflict among competitive ethical and moral values leaves us without a clear guide for conduct. Americans accept more violence in everyday life than other nationalities. Condoning violence is a pattern which characterizes us as a nation. We must strive toward awareness of its astronomical cost in dollars and its disastrous effect qualitatively throughout society. Juvenile violence is not receiving the attention it warrants. Crime has increased dramatically between the ages of ten and fourteen years. As Sandin says:

> the need for strengthening the moral fabric of American society has never been greater than at present. Momentous political and social questions are being addressed in our age, and an adequate moral framework for addressing these issues has become critical not only for the progress of civilization, but even, some would say, to the survival of the human race. (p. ix)

Sandin continues "despite the obvious urgency of the moral dilemmas confronting modern society, however, programs of values-related education remain fragmentary and unsystematic in most American education" (p. 3). He stresses that we are blind to values, which leads to lives of "value poverty" (p. 3). He believes that:

> the world in which we live is one of comparative affluence and enjoyment, but often our lives are impoverished in the midst of our abundance. A restricted sense of values prevents us from realizing our highest potential. (p. 3)

Sandin emphasizes that emptiness and monotony, as expounded by the intellectuals of the twentieth century, are not due to some newly discovered absurdity that exists in reality, but to spiritual blindness that prevents the attainment of deeper meanings. He states, "the present age has lost confidence in the process of moral judgment" (p. 4).

Development of moral maturity is a process of overcoming relativism and gaining reflective judgment concerning what kinds of actions and public policy will be most conducive to the human good. Virtue must be taught; it is not something we have at the time of birth. Virtue stresses that goodness inspires goodness, trust produces trustworthiness, and love creates love. It is our obligation to nurture virtue, to expect and foster responsible action, to insist on prudence, and to think about the actions necessary for attaining moral outcomes. Moral values are the basis for practical wisdom and virtue is the basis for a standard of excellence. The essence of moral thought is the relationship between virtue and the conditions under which a virtuous character can be developed. We must acknowledge the urgency to provide moral education, realizing that our schools and colleges are not well prepared for meeting this challenge. Values education, contrary to materialistic relativism, is essential. It is values that explain and give coherence to our judgments and define moral obligations. The fundamental goal is to assist people in becoming moral thinkers and to assist them in making moral decisions. It is precisely in this respect that we find prisoners to be deficient. Conscience training is imperative, not only in the prevention of criminal behavior, but for all aspects of moral living.

Empathetic feelings underlie the ability to engage in moral reasoning. This ability comes from attachments to parents and others who exemplify and teach love and understanding. Children learn to care and to distinguish right from wrong by internalizing the love they receive from others. Authorities agree that violence greatly impedes this process so moral values are not learned. Instead children learn to act out aggressively and behave impulsively. They become unduly vigilant and wary of the world. They misinterpret the actions of others and lash out because of their misperceptions. If they remain under stress, biological changes can occur and cause them to become unable to learn self-discipline. Violent behavior does not result from a single experience. It develops over a period of time by observing parents and other adults who are unable to control their aggressiveness. It is a gradual process that causes calm, self-inhibiting actions to be lost, leading to stubbornness and defiance, especially between the ages of eight and twelve years. Unfortunately, without treatment it results in anti-social conduct between twelve and fourteen years of age in the form of shoplifting, dealing in drugs, fighting, and defiance of authority. Studies show boys who have had good parental attachment and consistent discipline do not fall into this pattern. Parental interaction with their family prevents children from becoming involved in criminal activity.

Conscience and Crime

Special groups were selected for study in our investigation of conscience disorders. It was assumed that these groups might differ from normal in perception of right and wrong. One of these groups was comprised of men incarcerated because they had committed sex-offenses, mainly pedophiles. A segment of this study involved analysis of information about school achievement and ability to spell in written form. Those deficient in spelling reported poor success in learning to read and write. Approximately one-third of the pedophiles showed evidence of having learning disabilities. These results are significant in showing that many pedophiles have disorders that have persisted since childhood. Because of these learning disabilities they may have experienced school failure. By inference they have brain dysfunctions and different needs than those who are pedophiles but do not have such disabilities. Pedophiles cannot be considered homogeneous because they comprise sub-groups with specialized needs. Program planning must consider these differences. Pedophiles are not equivalent to those who rape or commit other sex-offenses.

Perhaps the most consequential of our results are those that show pedophiles vary in conscience function. They were less afraid of their conscience and find it to interfere less with self-esteem, which suggests that pedophiles have less arousal to right and wrong. They manifested less development of conscience so it is less effective in alerting them to the consequences of their actions. They might be designated as having a character disorder.

These results have implications for classification and treatment. It is typical to group all sex-offenders together and to plan treatment accordingly. This procedure may not be effective for those who have committed sex-offenses because the type of sex offense is critical to how they may be helped with their behavioral disorder. Pedophiles are deficient in conscience development and in need of assistance in discerning differences in right and wrong. Rapists and other sex-offenders, in contrast, are deficient in impulse control. They know what is right but are deficient in self-control or self-discipline. These behavioral disorders are not equivalent and treatment programs should not be identical. Only when these groups are separated and treatment planned specifically for each can we expect it to be most effective.

Pedophiles also have difficulties in emotional adjustment. About sixty percent said they felt they had failed in their daily pursuits. Presumably they were deficient in feelings of self-esteem. They expressed hope, however, with ninety percent saying they expected to change when they were released from prison. They showed remorse in that eighty-six percent said they would tell others not to do what they did, and eighty-eight percent said they felt guilty about what they had done. More than one-third reported they had been sexually abused in childhood.

Investigators have reported that pedophiles are angry while engaging in sex with children. In investigating this allegation we found twelve percent said sometimes they did not know whether they wanted sex or were just angry. When asked whether they felt angry while having sex only seven percent said yes. The extent to which anger is a factor is questionable; it cannot be considered a predominant feeling in pedophilia. More than half of the pedophiles said they felt helpless, expressing a serious level of anxiety about total well-being. This anxiety might be an important factor in treatment. Most of them said they were close to their mother in growing up; less than half said they were close to their father. This raises the question of sexual identity. The interview group was comprised of men between the ages of 21 and 70. Seven percent said they would rather be a woman. How this compares to a group of normal males is not known, but we cannot ignore the fact that sexual orientation may be an important factor in pedophilia. That they were close to their mothers in early life seems to support this observation. It is noteworthy one-third of them said they did not feel close to anyone.

Other parental factors are significant. Only about twenty percent reported they had been cautioned by their parents. In comparison more than two-thirds of the rapists and other sex offenders said their parents had told them what they were doing was wrong. We can only speculate as to why parents did not give more attention to their sons' molestation of children. It may not have been considered a serious trend or it may have been painful for parents to acknowledge what was happening. The pedophiles also showed poor success in marriage. Twice as many of them had been married and divorced in comparison with other sex-offenders.

Although the pedophiles and other sex-offenders vary in type of conscience dysfunction, both have difficulty in attaining the level of self-control necessary for everyday living. Reasons for lack of moral maturity are complex, but we emphasize that we give little attention to conscience training in our society. Children must be trained to understand that virtue is essential if life is to be lived in a fulfilling way. Its importance is implied by Mixon when he says, "today we lack a shared rationale or justification for morality" (p. 140). This admonition illustrates the significance of pursuing the study of conscience and stressing that nothing is more urgent than a renewed emphasis on conscience training by parents, educators, and others. We are not teaching moral values as we did in past generations. Instead there is opposition, emphasizing that values are detrimental to homogeneity. This point of view is in error. Without moral training and better understanding of the role of conscience, we can expect criminal behavior, chaos, disrespect, and aggression to increase. We are already witnessing increases in some types of crime and we have a burgeoning problem in our prisons. Much can be done to counteract these trends. Above all is the need to introduce training programs early in life to offset the trend to criminality by the age of fourteen years.

Sex-offenders represent one type of crime. There is need for better understanding and treatment for this group because sex offences are increasing and the harm to victims is incalculable. Also, sex-offenders present a different and serious problem, not only on the street but in prisons after they have been apprehended. This group, especially, must be understood as having conscience disorders with deficits in understanding moral issues. It is mainly in this way that they differ from other criminals, albeit morality is involved in all criminality.

Mixon states, "quite literally no one has authority to tell us what is right and what is wrong. Never in the history of the world has moral sovereignty been invested in each individual. Never before have people been so free to decide right from wrong" (p. 147). This freedom to think for ourselves is precious but along with it comes the responsibility for teaching moral values. Freedom to choose assumes understanding the moral choices that are most beneficial to all. We cannot use this freedom without first evaluating the moral implications. Moreover, freedom to choose assumes that standards for making beneficial choices have been established. Not all people acquire these standards and the consequences may be tragic. Raine has shown that criminals are deficient in social perception and unable to restrain anti-social impulses. He also says they do not develop a normal conscience, a position supported by our data. Raine emphasizes that "a well developed conscience is what holds many of us back from stealing even in those situations when we are almost certain of getting away with the theft undetected" (p. 216). Often we rely on tradition as a guide for social living and understanding. Tradition is informative and useful but, standing alone, it is inadequate as a self-control system. We need moral values, beliefs, and convictions if self-discipline is to be maintained. Conscience disorders are the most significant factor leading to violence and criminality.

CHAPTER V

A Study of Conscience

Being oblivious to moral values reflects emotional immaturity if not ignorance. We blame others for what is to our disadvantage and whatever impedes personal preference. This pattern is referred to as externalizing blame, a debilitating trend in our society. Blame is used to avoid responsibility for moral conduct; what occurs is the fault of others. When those who externalize blame are asked about wrongdoing, their response is one of indifference. They see nothing wrong with blaming the government, boss, company, church, neighbors, police, parents, schools, as well as other people and institutions. Butt made similar observations, "you shall not blame your neighbor for his short comings but name them a disease" (p. 118). He emphasizes that psychology promotes moral neutrality toward conditions formerly considered unacceptable. We have replaced "sin" with diseases, with little awareness of the consequences of this shift for individuals and society. The contradictions are seen when we call alcoholism a disease but drunk driving is judged to be a crime.

Psychology has been remiss in stressing the ill effects of guilt, assuming the individual is not at fault. McNeil suggests this relieves the person, but repudiates conscience and the need to assume responsibility, increasing human misery. He continues, "the attempt to relieve conscience is unrealistic; even if successful, man and society would be destroyed" (p. 325). To assume people do no wrong and refer to immoral conduct as being due to their condition is unacceptable.

What happened to responsibility? Moral conduct is not possible without it. Does this emphasis mean individuals should be denied basic freedoms? It does not. Undue supervision takes away the opportunity to be responsible. Being accountable for our conduct epitomizes the significance of moral values, the principles that serve as a basis for what we do. More and more we recognize the importance of conscience. Jones (1991) made a notable contribution in showing that psychoanalysis and religion can be complimentary. Although Freud viewed the most profound human sensibilities as components of lust and aggression, Jones says, "on the one hand, moral responsibility, especially the demands of truth, is the pinnacle of human maturity" (p. 2). He also says we have three relational needs: (1) the need to be connected to a greater, ideal reality; (2) the need for recognition and acceptance; (3) the need to experience others like us. Empathetic experience, he says, is the essence of interpersonal relationships, and "sanity and maturity require a moral ordering of life" (p. 37). In other words extreme secularization not only is detrimental to human beings, it is intolerable.

There are sacred aspects of life and we have the capability to be in touch with them. In considering these factors we are exploring our most fundamental experiences. In comparison with the secular, greatly emphasized in our age of technology, the sacred is not a trait nor an entity but an experience which is overpowering, awe inspiring, compelling, and inexhaustible. It leads to a mood of reverence and connects us with the foundations of our being. It underscores the idea that all who aspire to heightened self-awareness must be committed to something outside of themselves. Jones refers to this concept as the psychology of the sacred and admonishes that we "must recover the sacred buried within each of us" (p. 5). If we see others only as a way to gain something for ourselves, we have lost a part of what it means to be human. Only moral values make it possible to reflect our genuine humanity. But this aspect of being human is not emphasized. Rarely is conscience mentioned. Outlines for psychology courses reveal no description of this vital process. If it is mentioned it is referred to casually as though it is of little consequence. The emphasis is on a neutral, relativistic point of view. Each individual is to decide what is right for himself.

The foundation for a psychology of conscience is the concept of morality versus immorality. Cecil says conscience usually is an echo of religious faith. He believes much of what is emphasized in society is superficial and "greatness is achieved not by high standards of living but by standards of life based on moral values" (p. 177). An example is the legal system which cannot exist without a standard of morality. Cecil underscores that if science and technology are to enhance progress they must adhere to moral values which are "indispensable for social cohesion and spiritual progress" (p. 12). Without a moral agenda, the triumph promised by technology may only be a force for dehumanization and the domination of others. Personal integrity is the only basis for a moral, ethical world. Cecil believes "traditional moral values such as freedom, justice, prudence, love, fidelity, honesty, and other values were recognized by Plato, Aristotle, Moses and by Christ's teaching that the virtues which develop the whole man remain unchanged; they are the same today in the age of technology as they were yesterday" (p. 178). This is not commonly observed. Technology, it is assumed, is our only need. If it cannot be computerized it is viewed as being of little relevance. In fact, it is what cannot be computerized that forms the mainstay of what matters most. If those involved disregard honesty, for example, what is done in technology may be injurious, the basis for violent behavior. Only virtues can serve as a basis for successful, meaningful relationships and these virtues have not changed.

Despite references to conscience in popular literature there has been meager attention to it in academic circles. It is largely ignored in psychology. For this reason a Conscience Questionnaire to study how people perceive its role in their lives was developed (see Appendix). This Questionnaire consists of thirty-three items, half of which concern knowledge about conscience (information) and the other half how conscience is believed to have affected one's conduct (influence). Individuals respond by answering yes or no. Our purpose was to gather information on what people think about their conscience and how it influences their behavior. Although we do not hear much about this "arousal level," so fundamental to daily conduct, it is the primary basis for self-control. To give attention to what we are about we must be "aroused"; how and when we become aroused determines what we do about it. Arousal levels are basic to self-discipline and behavior in general. We might argue that our sensitivity to what is moral and what is immoral has diminished; that our guide for daily living is an attitude of "what is it that will give me an advantage or opportunity for personal gain."

The Questionnaire is a method for gathering information about the arousal level experienced by people in their everyday lives. It is a measure of how individuals feel about self-control and how successful they think they are in regulating themselves. Significant work on the meaning and importance of self-regulation has been reported by Baumeister, Heatherton, and Tice. They show that there are basic psychological processes that make up this aspect of everyone's life. They found attention is a primary factor; if self-control is not attended to, nothing can be done about it. Conscience holds the key because it serves as the system that alerts us to the morality of what we are doing. Preoccupation may cause us to lose control. Baumeister, Heatherton, and Tice found the ability to see beyond the immediate is fundamental in self-regulation. Conscience plays a predominant role because of its importance in what is considered significant beyond immediate experience.

Arousal level, therefore, is primary to successful self-control. If we are not aroused and attentive to our conduct and the conduct of others we cannot engage in self-evaluation or self-monitoring. This concept is the basis for our study of conscience. We believe it is conscience that determines our level of arousal and the Conscience Questionnaire was developed to study this process. We studied eight groups of people: liberal arts, university and seminary students, senior citizens, Lutheran clergy, prisoners, and Japanese and Mexican college students, a total of about one thousand people. These groups differed on many items, sometimes showing arousal levels that differed significantly. A brief discussion is given concerning these differences item by item. The lowest arousal level was manifested by prisoners, a finding of great significance in understanding criminal behavior. Another consistent finding was that Mexican students differed widely from the other groups on most items, sometimes falling at a level opposite from other groups.

The Results of the Conscience Questionnaire

Were You Born With a Conscience

One might assume that beliefs about the origin of conscience are related to how its relevance is perceived. Comparison by group revealed differences. Approximately two-thirds of the total group surveyed believe that we are born with a conscience in a manner comparable to skin color. We assume this means they believe it is a fixed entity; there is nothing that can be done about it. This is contrary to our point of view. Conscience is not a fixed entity, and every parent, teacher, and adult has responsibility for helping youth develop this self-regulation system. If conscience were inborn, its function might be fixed and one's arousal level would not be variable, not a function of training. Consideration of conscience in relation to conduct should include awareness of these results because they reveal the problem before us, the massive task of developing an arousal level, in providing instruction concerning conscience and its purpose in our lives. Although almost everyone recognizes conscience, understanding its vital role in self-discipline is lacking. A first step is for parents to become aware of their responsibility in providing the training that makes conscience possible. Parental home training should be enhanced, especially in churches and synagogues.

Is Conscience a Universal Human Characteristic

How we view conscience serves as the background for how we view ourselves and others. When we realize that conscience is a dynamic process which provides a basis for self-discipline we have a standard for self-evaluation and for understanding others. Recognizing that conscience plays a significant role in everyone's life gives us insights that are far-reaching.

The purpose of this question was to ascertain whether people believe everyone has a conscience even though they may give no attention to it nor be aware of it. Except for the Mexicans there is considerable agreement that conscience is a universal human characteristic. The Japanese more than other groups hold this opinion. Of the Americans, prisoners score lowest. Seminarians and clergymen believe that conscience is universal.

In comparing these responses with the first question a contradiction appears. If we believe conscience is inborn it seems that we would also believe it is universal. However, this logical inference cannot be made. Two-thirds of the Japanese said conscience is inborn, but 94% said it was universal. Similarly, more Americans believe conscience is universal than say it is inborn. Of the Mexicans slightly more than 50% believe we are born with a conscience, but none believe it is universal.

Why these discrepancies? Perhaps these results simply indicate a low level of understanding of conscience, its meaning intellectually, emotionally, and spiritually. Simplistic notions about conscience are prevalent everywhere. Black states "moralism is a product of its social environment" (p. 44). The implication is that moral values are relative, there are no standards except what a given society permits or prohibits. But moral values including religious and spiritual values are often in opposition to what society condones. A mature conscience is based on moral values that society may or may not emulate. Black also says moralism is rigid and uncompromising. When violence, criminality, and injustice are involved, moral values are uncompromising and do not permit acceptance of such conduct as a model to be followed. Moral conduct does not mean intolerance, impatience, or poor understanding of others. On the contrary, moral values include kindness, respect, flexibility, independence, and accountability. Moralists want rules established by society through laws that foster and strengthen moral values, not impede or distort them. So the question of the universality of conscience underlies virtually all aspects of life and relates to the overall question of arousal levels as they pertain to everyone. It remains for us to learn more about why people believe conscience is not universal, how conscience is related to conduct irrespective of race and nationality. With more study of this process we will gain insights into how shared moral beliefs lead to tolerance and maintenance of peace throughout the world.

Conscience is unique to human beings. Although it may be undeveloped or disturbed, it is a major characteristic separating humans from other forms of animal life. Hence, one's belief about the universality of conscience reflects one's view of people, of humanity and the obligation to foster values.

Does Conscience Represent Only What You Were Told as a Child

The origin of conscience has been studied in various ways. Viewing conscience as a process that determines arousal level adds to its significance because it raises questions concerning how we attain self-discipline. Do we gain understanding of ourselves developmentally or is self-regulation determined only by what we were told in childhood? We have emphasized that conscience develops as the result of instruction and discipline by parents but is this its only basis? If conscience is only a set of rules ingrained in childhood then conduct is regulated only by this set of regulations and we grow into adulthood learning to abide by them. This belief differs widely from the one we propose: conscience develops gradually and is an ongoing active process.

Our results show that how one views this question varies by culture and race, with implications for how one views the development of self-discipline. Mexicans see these aspects of conduct as being based on rules learned as children and view conscience as a fixed entity, a set of rules to be learned and followed throughout life. We can argue that this means internal controls are less necessary or even irrelevant. Self-control consists of following early-life rules and regulations. To some extent this is true also of the Japanese, but from other evidence we find they are dependent on rules given by the group to which they belong, not only internal controls.

Americans believe conscience is acquired developmentally, the result of training and discipline over a period of time. Presumably, this means they view conscience more as a dynamic process dependent on the training children and youth receive. This belief puts responsibility on parents to provide the discipline needed. If conscience is viewed only as what we have been told as children, one's arousal level and alertness to wrong doing is a fixed characteristic. If training is not received in childhood self-control cannot be attained.

Arousal level is a significant feature of moral conduct and is determined by how well conscience functions. Despite differences by race and culture its role in self-control cannot be ignored. Its developmental nature needs to be emphasized and its role as the basis for self-discipline recognized. Conscience is a dynamic process that functions throughout life.

Does Your Conscience Represent What You Believe to be Right or Wrong

Conscience serves as the basis for maintaining self-control. Through its arousal we learn whether what we do is right or wrong. This question concerns the function of conscience and involves our value system, whether conscience represents these values and makes arousal possible.

Conscience is perceived by most Americans as a self-monitoring system, but differences appear on the basis of race and culture. Only slightly more than half of the Japanese view conscience in this way. Many Japanese believe what is right and wrong is determined by society rather than by an individual's internal standards. This seems to be the point of view held by Doi who observes, "what is characteristic about the Japanese sense of guilt is that it shows itself most sharply when the individual suspects that his action will result in betraying the group to which he belongs" (p. 49). However, many Japanese, like Americans, believe conscience represents values, standards for what is judged to be right or wrong. There are major differences within the Japanese population concerning the function of conscience. This difference is larger than within the American population where more than 90% believe that conscience is the system that represents right and wrong.

Mexicans differed widely from Americans, only about one-fourth of them saying conscience represents what they believe to be right and wrong. They believe conscience is inborn, not a universal human characteristic, and only what we have been told in childhood. On this question concerning whether conscience represents what we believe to be right and wrong about 77% of them said no. It seems Mexicans do not believe internalized standards form the basis for values. Rather, what is judged as right and wrong is due to other factors such as rules applied by society.

Mexicans, and to some extent the Japanese, do not believe conscience is the system that arouses us to what is right. It is not clear how they make judgments except that the Japanese rely on standards established by the group to which they belong. Mexicans appear to depend on rules given in early life. It may be that these rules are enhanced by the church and that this is one of the external influences that assists them in right and wrong judgments.

Is Conscience Related to Religious Beliefs

It is possible to have a conscience regardless of beliefs about God, but religious beliefs have implications for moral conduct. Batson, Schoenrade, and Ventis suggest that the sincerity of beliefs must be evaluated. These investigators found some people engage in religious practices to gain advantages and to impress those from whom they hope to benefit. Some individuals have intrinsic religious beliefs; the belief per se motivates them and is the foundation of their convictions. Those who engage in religious practices for external, self-serving reasons in comparison with the irreligious show no differences in behavior. Those who have intrinsic religious beliefs are different in that they are more likely to be unprejudiced, behave morally, and lead lives of caring and service with feelings of worth and well-being. Infancy is the period during which feelings of trust are initiated and when mistrust takes over conscience development may be impaired. This is a serious consideration because feelings of hope depend upon trustworthiness.

The question, "is conscience related to religious beliefs," was included to explore the understanding persons have about this self-regulation process. Allport (1955) stresses that conscience often is referred to as the "voice of God." Others emphasize different facets, such as Lehman who states, "conscience is the bond between duty and obligation" (p. 33). He quotes Thomas Aquinas: "conscience is a human device for spot-checking right from wrong" (p. 33). In the Judeo-Christian religion conscience is frequently mentioned as a monitor of moral conduct. Although conscience is important in religious beliefs, it is not the direct result of such beliefs. It is not the product of a given religion nor is it exclusively a religious phenomenon. Indirectly, this question again raises the issue of the origin of conscience.

Americans respond that conscience is related to religious beliefs, but prisoners varied in that only slightly more than half hold this view. Why do most prisoners not recognize the relationship between conscience and religious beliefs? We might conclude that trust and feelings of worth did not develop normally during infancy. If this is true we would expect their feelings of hope, caring, and service would be less mature, with less ability to use moral reasoning, in support of findings reported by Raine.

The Japanese and Mexicans again differ from Americans; less than half saying conscience and religious beliefs are related. These results are similar to others suggesting racial and cultural patterns are influential in the perception of conscience, its origin, and function; rules governing conduct are less related to internal value standards, including religious beliefs. However, we should not equate Japanese and Mexicans because results show they vary greatly from each other. The Japanese vary from Americans in different ways than do the Mexicans. The Japanese are more other-directed in gaining self-esteem whereas the Americans are more inner-directed.

Is the Conscience of Children the Same as that of Adults

To understand conscience, to be in position to use it effectively, and to help others in its development, it is necessary to consider its function. One way to gain the knowledge we need is to analyze the role of conscience in children as compared to adults. We have suggested that conscience is not inborn, but capacity for its development is present at birth. The question, "is the conscience of children the same as that of adults," relates to other questions about origin and development. If conscience is inborn developmental aspects would be limited. Because we believe it must be developed through training we do not assume that the conscience of children is the same as that of adults. If improperly developed the result is youth and adults who are conscienceless, with implications for ruthless conduct and criminality. Children who have not developed a conscience have no internalized values which can be aroused. Not having a conscience means that self-regulation is impossible. Through instruction, training, and discipline the self-regulation system begins to evolve early in life. Without proper training this system cannot develop, causing individuals to have the greatest handicap possible. Some individuals believe we are less successful in helping youth in development of self-control than in former years.

Of the groups surveyed the Mexicans differ most remarkably from the others. Almost all of them saying the conscience of children is the same as adults. Their response is identical to the question of whether conscience is only what we are told as children. Mexicans seem to believe conscience is comprised of what children are told in childhood and remains the same throughout life. They do not believe conscience develops over a period of time but is a fixed characteristic at birth and does not change. In all probability this belief influences what they perceive as the role of parents in the moral training of children. As noted earlier, they view such training as a process of learning the rules in early life and abiding by them. Accordingly, they see conscience and internalized standards as being of less consequence.

Comparison of results for this question with those from other items is revealing. Americans overwhelmingly believe the conscience of children and adults are not the same. This response includes perception of how conscience functions. If one believes conscience is inborn it might follow that consideration of developmental aspects would not be important. But such logical inferences cannot be made. Except for the Mexicans the belief that the conscience of children and adults is not the same is held much more strongly than the belief it is inborn. There is awareness that conscience develops from childhood into adulthood. This indicates recognition that children cannot be expected to show arousal for what is wrong and must be given training for the development of self-control. Only when conscience develops can we expect arousal levels to be adequate for self-appraisal and self-regulation. These levels should be evaluated in youth who are prone to criminality as well as in all prisoners. When conscience has not been adequately established every effort should be made to foster its development because self-control is dependent on it.

Do You Listen to Your Conscience

When conscience arouses us to the meaning of our conduct we might give attention to the message or we might ignore it. Much depends on whether we take the information seriously. The question, "do you listen to your conscience," was intended to provide evidence about how people respond to their conscience. Do they treat this information as significant?

It is not unusual to hear comments about conscience in expressions such as "my conscience bothers me," or as that "still small voice." These expressions connote an audible experience as though their conscience is talking to them. We did not intend this question to imply that a voice is heard. Our purpose was to gain information about how individuals react to the arousal that conscience provides. Are these signals generally recognized or ignored?

Americans surveyed, except for criminals, uniformly state they listen to the messages received. These results indicate that criminals have a less functional conscience in comparison with normal groups. It is essential that treatment programs for criminals include evaluation of conscience together with training programs to raise arousal levels. Punitive measures alone are inadequate.

The Japanese responses again varied from the American, about one-fourth saying they did not listen to their conscience. There are similarities between the Japanese and Americans but there is less uniformity among the Japanese. They rely more on group or social controls. Self-discipline is gained more from sources other than internalized values.

By far the greatest group difference appeared for Mexicans; more than 90% said they do not listen to their conscience. Their perception of conscience and its functions varies considerably from Americans. They rely on external rules, mainly provided in childhood, to serve as the governing influence for conduct. If one relies on external authority as the guide for daily decisions there is no need to listen to the signals provided by conscience. The need to acquire internalized standards is negated. The standards followed are derived from rules provided by external authority.

Does Your Conscience Help You

Perhaps most persons do not think about their conscience as being helpful. But there are reasons for raising this question. It concerns feelings about whether our conduct abides by the moral values we have internalized. Some people may not prefer to have these admonitions, especially if they result from a punitive conscience. Because of the role conscience has in maintaining integrity we should cherish this process at the highest level of our aspirations. To be without a normally functioning conscience is to be unable to appreciate what it means to be human. Conscience is not only helpful, but essential to all aspects of our lives. A disordered conscience causes conflict in the development of values.

With the exception of the Mexicans all groups agree that conscience is helpful. These results indicate that most people realize the significance of conscience as an arousal system. Again, however, criminals are lowest; we have seen from responses on other items that their awareness and understanding of conscience is below normal. This trend implies that criminals would be better understood if conscience were used as a criterion for evaluating their conduct. More than 90% of the Mexicans stated that conscience is not helpful. If Mexicans rely mainly on external controls they would not find conscience to be helpful; they might even view it as being detrimental.

Does Your Conscience Cause You to Feel Shameful

Feeling shameful cannot be separated from a normally functioning conscience. It is one of the feelings that derive from the arousal process, but is specific to perception of how others judge us. Shame serves a purpose and should not be thought of negatively. It can and does serve to help us with self-control even though at times this feeling may get out of hand.

All of those surveyed said conscience caused them to have feelings of shame but there were differences among the groups. Of the Americans the criminals feel the least shame. They are less sensitive to messages from conscience; another indication of why they became criminals. Other Americans report their conscience causes them to feel shameful, with university students having the highest level of these feelings, followed by senior citizens, liberal arts students and clergymen.

The Japanese and Mexicans were equivalent with approximately half of each group saying their conscience causes them to feel shameful. Both the Japanese and Mexicans experience less shame than Americans. This might be expected inasmuch as these groups, especially the Mexicans, show less reliance on internalized standards. Doi provides a helpful explanation when he states not conscience, but fear of dishonor and being ostracized by one's group is the greatest shame one can experience in Japanese society. Japanese are more "other directed" in their personal relationships. Their conscience is less likely to cause feelings of shame.

The results for this question add credence to the argument that feelings of shame are a normal manifestation of a working conscience. There are times when such feelings should be expected. The issue is not whether these feelings should occur, but how we react and manage them. It is the role of conscience to cause us to feel shameful under certain circumstances. This is one of the ways conscience provides us with the arousal we need. When we recognize these feelings for what they are we use them to help differentiate between right and wrong.

Does Your Conscience Represent Your Values

Almost everyone realizes conscience is related to guilt, shame, and remorse. But its consequences are much broader. Values form the basis of character and judgments concerning moral relevance. They determine our choices. If we reject values, we reject conscience and encourage immorality. The implications are far-reaching and involve distinguishing between good and evil and between health and survival. Ours is an era in which values and morality are controversial and emphasizes the concept that all is relative. We need to renew old values and originate new ones, not only on the basis of new knowledge, but because of circumstances associated with technological innovations. Science has improved our daily lives but it has also revealed that science alone cannot meet all emotional and spiritual needs. Purpose and spiritual meaning must be included in socio-cultural patterns or we become depersonalized, even victimized by greed and avarice.

Perhaps without full awareness most people associate conscience with values, but do not realize it is the system that serves as the center for internalized standards. A primary function of conscience is to represent values and to alert us to them in a constant, ongoing way. Conscience not only represents values, it signals us when behavior impinges upon them. It is of considerable interest, therefore, to see the results for this question. Except for prisoners, Americans are in close agreement that conscience represents values. Most of the prisoners also hold this belief but to a lesser extent. They are less aware of what conscience means, that it is the system that provides the basis for self-control; they are less able to distinguish between right and wrong and have less well established moral standards. The Japanese responded similarly but at a lower level; 90% of Americans said conscience represented their values as compared to 76% of Japanese.

Mexican responses were opposite from the others with 83% saying conscience does not represent their values. Compared with Americans and Japanese their perception of conscience varies widely. We have seen that Mexicans rely less on internalized value standards and more on external influences. It is consistent, therefore, that they do not perceive conscience as a value system.

Do You Bribe Your Conscience

Conscience cannot function without making demands. We cannot attain self-control without responding when conscience arouses us. We are always under scrutiny of this system, for better or for worse. Most people learn to take these warnings without feelings of pessimism or distress. But some find arousal by conscience troublesome, wanting to eliminate these signals. In so doing, they often become victims of gambling, drugs, and alcohol. When such conscience disorders prevail the attempt is to subdue all signals from conscience. Sometimes this takes the form of bribes. Perhaps everyone uses bribes to manage the demands of conscience. Such efforts may be appropriate under some circumstances, but often lead to loss of control with serious consequences.

Use of bribes is of great concern in the home and workplace. Bribing ourselves involves self-deceit. People are not aware of how dishonest they are with themselves. A working conscience means we are sensitive to values and want to maintain the standards we have established. We must recognize that anything we do to make signals from conscience go away means we face loss of self-regulation with consequences that can be devastating. When this awareness is weak we are tempted to give in to desires that may not only be humiliating but injurious. Giving in to these desires means we must do something that relinquishes the demands of conscience and we do this by bribing it. There are innumerable ways in which we come up with explanations to ourselves intended to relieve the warnings we receive from conscience. A problem arises when bribing becomes a way to overlook values. If this pattern predominates we become self-centered, indulgent, and criminally inclined, comparable to those who are conscienceless.

The question, "do you bribe your conscience," raises the issue of moral values, how we respond to the standards we have acquired. We would expect those with strong moral standards to resist using bribes and respond favorably when alerted by conscience. In fact there may be a continuum that applies to people ranging from those who rarely use bribes to those who use them routinely and engage in immorality. The results from our survey suggest this pattern. It is surprising to find about half of the American students and clergy say they bribe their conscience. There are many people who deal with the messages from conscience by reducing their urgency or eliminating them. The senior citizens also fall into this category, with one-third saying they used such bribes. The criminals felt less need to "outwit" conscience through bribery. They have lower internalized standards so they feel "pangs" of conscience to a lesser extent than non-criminals; again, an indication of why they are criminals.

The Mexican and Japanese students scored similarly on this question with two-thirds saying they bribe their conscience, which means they use bribery as a technique more than the Americans. We have seen that the Japanese, because of their reliance on standards maintained by their group, might not feel that the messages from conscience are as relevant to what they do as the Americans, so bribing is a matter of alleviating a secondary process in their adjustment. The Mexicans place minimal credence on conscience and deal with its messages as being of superficial significance.

If we think of bribing as an attempt to circumvent the demands of conscience, we can say about one-half of Americans and two-thirds of Japanese and Mexicans use this process. These results are challenging. Why do so many people find they must use bribery to manage their conscience? Assuming this is not due to conscience disorders, it indicates an immaturity of conscience; not the best circumstance for internalizing value standards. When one-half to two-thirds find it necessary to alleviate conscience demands in this way, we see a need for further study of this process. What is the nature of these bribes? Are they related to moral behavior, addiction, child abuse, or other types of self-control failure? Bribery is a deficiency in self-regulation for which remedial procedures should be developed.

Are You Afraid of Your Conscience

When we receive messages from conscience our response may be to see it as a signal to alter our conduct. But this is not always the case. Some people's responses are characterized by feelings of guilt, shame, and remorse, while others react mainly with fear. Why do some people become afraid when their conscience warns them? There are many reasons but perhaps paramount is that they feel if they do not conform they will be rejected. Such feelings are anxiety-producing. Individuals who have a normal conscience have no fear about what it tells them, but experience arousal from the messages. However, if arousal becomes a pattern it is indicative of a conscience disorder. We can assume these feelings range from mild to severe. If it is severe it is seriously inhibiting and causes withdrawal, extreme caution, and hesitancy because the person is insecure in what he says and does. Those who are afraid of their conscience have difficulty in relating to others and feel alienated.

Conscience fears occur for various reasons but the predominant one is the use of punitive discipline by parents. Straus has shown that spanking children (use of violence) causes a sense of powerlessness and "lack of internalized moral values" (p. 145). Magid and McKelvey found that when disciplinary techniques interfered with bonding it caused boys to be self-destructive and cruel. Punitiveness underlies fear of conscience because throughout childhood conscience represents parental authority. Fear of conscience, therefore, is fear of authority and of living up to what is expected. When these fears cause anxiety to the extent that it hampers personal success the situation must be dealt with therapeutically.

Our results show that fear of conscience is common. More than one-third of senior citizens express this fear showing that even late in life it is prevalent. Of the groups surveyed, seminarians and pastors are least fearful and college students and prisoners fall in the middle range. About one-third of Americans say they are afraid of their conscience. To ignore such fears is detrimental to conscience development. Further study of criminals would be revealing because they did not follow the trend of being below normal. Why are many of them afraid of their conscience? Does this fear correlate with types of criminality? Our data do not provide a basis for conclusions, but it is unlikely that all who fear conscience fall within the limits of normal. We assume a segment of this group have fears falling at the level of severe, with emotional disturbances that hamper their daily lives. The arousal level experienced might cause anxiety, distractibility, restlessness, worry, and stress to the extent of jeopardizing good health.

The findings for the Japanese are also revealing, about one-fourth saying they are afraid of their conscience, compared to one-third of Americans. The Mexicans present a special case with the number who say they are afraid of their conscience being much greater than any other group. Inasmuch as they said conscience as an internalized value system is of less relevance than expressed by other groups, why are so many of them afraid of it? Despite their different perception of conscience and its relevance they fear this process that alerts them to being moral persons. Perception of authority may be involved. Although they seem to associate authority with rules given in childhood, they may have fears about living up to what is expected.

Conclusions must be tentative, but within our society there is apprehension about conscience and its function. Further study of these feelings would be helpful in bringing about better understanding of conscience, how it is a key to developing the moral values critical to everyone's well-being. As an aspect of humanness conscience should not be feared.

Does Your Conscience Interfere With Feelings of Self-Esteem

Self-esteem leads to confidence and causes us to act differently than if troubled with self-doubt. Scharzer has shown that people with feelings of self-worth are more likely to be successful. Blatt and Homan found that when we feel we are being avoided or neglected feelings of self-worth suffer. It is difficult to maintain feelings of self-esteem if we do not have a normally functioning conscience. If conscience causes us to have levels of arousal that are either too high or too low we cannot make decisions to direct daily activities, leading to doubt and anxiety. Unfortunately, many individuals do not recognize that conscience is related to feelings of self-esteem.

The results for this question are unusual. Of all groups senior citizens, more than any other, say conscience disturbs feelings of self-esteem; 70% said yes. Are they more sensitive than other groups? Are their arousal levels higher than they should be? We have seen that this group tends to respond at a higher level than others. Being a senior citizen does not necessarily mean conscience is no longer of consequence to peace of mind. Better understanding of this process would be an advantage for this group as well as for the others.

Except for the Japanese the groups responded uniformly with about half saying conscience interferes with self-esteem. These results include Mexicans and prisoners; this is one of the few instances in which Mexicans did not differ from Americans.

Although Mexicans perceive conscience in a widely different way, its effect on emotional well-being is not different, with half of them finding conscience interferes with self-esteem. If we assume this means that conscience is troublesome, this conflict is the same for Americans and Mexicans.

The Japanese differ from Americans and Mexicans with only 29% saying conscience interferes with self-esteem. Japanese, who rely largely on group identification, feel less conflict with self-esteem. Condon provides an illuminating discussion of how Japanese differ from Americans. He says, "in countless ways both obvious and subtle, the Japanese are encouraged to think first of being part of a group. We always comes before *I*—we of this family, we of this nation, or just we who are in this room talking. One is never fully independent, one must always be conscious of others" (p. 9). For Japanese self-esteem relates mainly to being successful in group relationships so conscience and self-esteem are not as closely related as when they serve as the primary basis for self-control. Even when Japanese are away from their group it is essential that they maintain good relations with it. They are responsible for not having conflict with others so they try not to embarrass their group. That which is humiliating and produces anxiety derives mainly from how they are accepted by the group, not from an internalized behavior standard.

Except for the Japanese more than half of those surveyed say conscience interferes with feelings of self-esteem. Should so many of us have this conflict? Questions might be raised concerning whether these results indicate an immaturity of conscience development. If conscience and its functions were more adequately understood this conflict might be alleviated. Having a mature conscience does not imply it should hamper emotional maturity, including feelings of self-esteem. It means conflicts are under control so no disadvantageous emotional consequences occur. These results are indicative of an immature conscience, not at the level of a disorder but at a level that reveals need for greater awareness of what is involved in having a normal self-control process.

Does Your Conscience Cause You to Feel Anxious

Anxiety is sometimes referred to as the scourge of our era, but it is rare for psychologists to study the association between conscience and anxiety, feelings of dread and being threatened. The feeling is not fear of physical threat but of punishment, being rejected, and of not being loved. These feelings lead to illness, as shown by Martin and Carlson who studied people under stress. They found that spiritually oriented persons perceive stress-inducing demands as being less upsetting and experience fewer health consequences than those who are not spiritually oriented. Neglect of what is morally obligatory often causes anxiety and depression. When we violate conscience it is referred to as sin, but professionals refer to violation of the superego as guilt. Any indiscretion concerning conscience may produce conflicts that lead to anxiety. A poorly developed conscience is not uncommon. Allport (1951) states, "the adult conscience is expected to have adult stature and escape entirely from the habit structure of childhood" (p. 89). Unfortunately, because so little attention has been given to this human characteristic this expectation is far from being achieved, with dire consequences at all levels of society. Violence and conscience are closely related. A mature conscience is dominated by positive goals, feelings of obligation toward others, and a perception of life as a mission with purpose and meaning. Conscience is the center for meaning and for the moral values cherished as guidelines for everyday life. A disordered conscience causes emotional turmoil including anxiety. Fear and dread are indicators of a punitive conscience or one sick in other ways. In helping those with emotional problems we cannot overlook the association between conscience and generalized anxiety.

Our survey revealed conscience to be anxiety producing for many people but there are differences by group. Again it is not clear why senior citizens experience anxiety about what is morally right and wrong. Perhaps sensitivity to moral issues increases with age so arousal levels reach their maximum at this time of life; the data on conscience by age supports this possibility. But the question of whether senior citizens are overly aroused remains to be further investigated. The clergy are least anxious, followed by prisoners. Presumably pastors have resolved conflicts involving conscience so they have less cause for anxiety concerning moral issues. The circumstances for the prisoners is much different. Prisoners showing less anxiety about moral questions is indicative of their low arousal levels relative to right and wrong conduct.

About 70% of American students say their conscience causes them to feel anxious, which suggests many youth have concerns about values and are struggling with issues of moral living. We do not know the severity of their anxiety, but these results indicate a need for better understanding of conscience. If conscience were given the attention it warrants there would be less fear of it and understanding of morally responsible goals would be greatly enhanced.

The Japanese show the least anxiety about conscience. The Mexicans fell close to the average for Americans. As in the case of self-esteem, although the Mexicans perceive conscience differently, the effect on their feelings is comparable to Americans. When conscience causes one to feel anxious we suspect that there is a fear of internalized authority. If this is true it appears to be a common feeling. Anxiety can be debilitating so there is a need for better understanding of how it can be relieved.

Does Your Conscience Cause You to Feel Depressed

If one's conscience is troublesome it might lead to depression. When arousal levels are high one of the first reactions is anxiety—"why am I worrying so much?" This is followed by depression—"I can never live up to what I want to be." When such feelings are severe, major emotional disturbances occur. Avoidance of decisions regarding moral values is not the answer. Lewis reminds us:

> The study of values might once have been of primarily individual concern and deliberation as to how to live a good life. Today it is a matter of collective human survival. If we identify the study of human values as a branch of philosophy, then the time has arrived for women and men to become philosophers—or else. (p. ix)

Conscience causes depression when we have confused values. It is we who are confused, the values in themselves are not muddled. We have failed to recognize that we must devote the time, thought, and energy necessary to make choices that result in moral living. To prevent depression and other conscience disorders we must be aware that "a mature conscience is one which is willing to risk the responsibility of committing itself to action based on norms which are reasonable and sane, but do not always claim to be infallible and of invariable validity" (Merton, p. 125). Merton observes "our varied ethical principles tend to become extremely hazy and even entirely forgotten or discredited" (p. 129). Conscience is relevant to all aspects of our lives.

When we experience depression because of remorse about what we have done, or not done, we should raise questions about our conscience. Is our arousal level so high we find ourselves in a state of concern much of the time? If so, we need assistance in modifying our conscience. We should expect conflicts regarding values because they are ever present in moral living. It is when they do not occur that we face tenuous and dangerous situations. The interaction of conscience and depression is of importance as shown by the results from our survey.

Americans respond uniformly, with more than half saying conscience causes them to feel depressed. The seminarians were lowest with one-third saying yes. The criminals were not significantly different from the others. Of all groups the Japanese were lowest and Mexicans highest. Two-thirds of Mexicans say conscience causes them to feel depressed. Although they perceive conscience in a different way compared to Americans, the effect of conscience on their emotional well-being is considerable. However, we must keep these results in perspective. More than half of the Americans also report feelings of depression caused by conscience. Why do people have such feelings? We are not doing well in the development of a mature conscience. We have no regular programs of instruction for its development. This vital aspect of well-being is essentially ignored.

Does Your Conscience Cause You to Feel Remorse

Questions concerning remorse are usually raised in connection with criminal behavior. Some individuals who commit serious crimes show no remorse, seemingly oblivious to the horrendous nature of what they have done. Lack of remorse is a criterion in planning treatment because unless criminals have insight about the cruelty of their conduct, it is unlikely they will benefit from rehabilitation efforts. Without evidence of a working conscience, a possibility of a mental disorder must be considered.

We chose to raise this question because some who feel remorse are not necessarily depressed or anxious. Like anxiety and depression, remorse is not an all or nothing feeling. It may be intense or essentially lacking. There is always conflict, if not pain, when one strives to live morally, but the advantages are indescribable compared to a life of immorality. However, exaggerated feelings of remorse may lead to physical illness. It is normal to feel remorse when we have done something not in harmony with moral values. These feelings should not be ignored. They are messages from conscience, our sensitivity has been aroused, and we should be aware of what is happening. Peace of mind, the greatest of all gifts, does not mean we will never experience conflict. It means we recognize feelings for what they are, a part of what it means to be human, that all experience can be meaningful and enhance moral living.

The question of remorsefulness raises other issues concerning conscience. For example, why do some people feel remorseful and some do not? When remorse is intense conscience may be sending erroneous messages or it may be sending messages that are needed. In the first instance arousal levels are in excess of what is beneficial and in the second case arousal levels are not attained. These complex issues must be included in the discussion of conscience. There are dangers either way. Normal feelings of remorse are characteristic of humanness. To show remorse means we are sensitive to right and wrong, with the result that conscience informs us of a transgression. Without feelings of empathy and caring, we would not have feelings of remorse. Feelings of remorse reveal a desire to do what is needed to compensate for actions that were offensive, if not detrimental to ourselves as well as to others. Individuals who cannot show these feelings are untrustworthy and sometimes dangerous.

Because feelings of remorse are fundamental to survival the results from our survey are of particular interest. Americans respond uniformly with two-thirds saying conscience caused them to feel remorse. But the association between conscience and feelings of remorse may be troublesome to some people. Of the two-thirds who find conscience causes them to feel remorseful, we assume that for some these feelings are intense and cause hardships emotionally. We need to bring this possibility to the attention of professionals so those in need of assistance can be served.

Mexicans respond in a different way; two-thirds report that conscience does not cause remorse. Although they say conscience causes them to feel anxious and depressed they do not feel remorse. This is in contrast to the Japanese who feel little depression, but three-fourths say conscience causes them to feel remorseful. If the Japanese embarrass their group they have remorse and feel restitution must be made.

Normal feelings of remorse seem basic to conduct and interpersonal relationships. By a large majority Americans and Japanese have this feeling. If Mexicans adhere mainly to rules learned in childhood, as compared to internalized values learned throughout life, it may be that remorse is less useful in relation to internalized standards.

Remorse tells us how well we fulfill obligations, in contrast to the relativistic point of view which emphasizes that internalized standards are not to be trusted. As Merton says, "we desperately need to talk and think, more candidly and more intelligently, about personal morality, now as perhaps never before" (p. xvii). He defines morality as strength of character. We are in control of our lives to the extent that we adhere to moral values, which requires that we understand the meaning of remorse. We must tolerate these feelings of arousal, be aware of them as messages, and understand their significance.

Is It Possible To Follow Your Conscience In Everyday Life

How we think about conscience influences what we do. If we think of it as irrelevant we cannot be sensitive to the signals it provides. Conscience is not simply an ethereal, mystical feature in our lives. It is an essential process that relates us to every other person and provides us with needed guidance. In raising the question about following our conscience our purpose was to gather information on how much we trust this system that integrates experience. Are the messages we receive reliable indications of how to conduct ourselves or are they only a means for generating anger, anxiety, and hostility? These questions are pertinent to the premise that conscience is the basis for our ability to control violence and to show love. This question also concerns the depth of our commitment to moral values. If we ignore conscience even though we may claim to be moral, we are hypocritical, saying one thing but doing something in conflict, an indication of lack of integrity. We cannot expect perfection because there are always instances in which what we profess and what we do are in conflict. But it is not these exceptions that are of major concern. It is the pattern of behavior that we must be aware of. If we only occasionally conform to our moral standards, we must realize that we are weak in character. On the other hand when our pattern is to be honest, tolerant, patient, and caring we show that we subscribe to these values and adhere to them.

In responding to this question several factors are involved. If the response is positive the implication is that one can live by his moral values in a realistic manner and that conscience is a useful guide to daily conduct. This positive attitude is reflected in the results because more than two-thirds of the Americans say it is possible to follow conscience in everyday life. Most Japanese also show this conviction about their conscience. Moreover, the Mexicans scored similarly, almost identical to the university students. It is difficult to know how confident we can be about the optimistic nature of these results in view of the level of violence and corruption around us. However, irrespective of culture and race there is agreement that one can follow his conscience in everyday life. This seems in contrast with the confusion in many circles, not only with youth, but in adults throughout a wide age range.

Why are these confusions not readily apparent in our results? One reason may be that those surveyed responded only in terms of possibilities. They may be saying one should follow his moral standards, but may not necessarily do so. Whatever the total meaning of these findings, it is of interest that people agree that moral values are reliable and that they can serve as a guide in daily living, irrespective of having a different perception of conscience.

Does Your Conscience Interfere With Peace of Mind

One of the most common statements heard about conscience is that it is troublesome. Many people have difficulty living with their conscience, sometimes to the extent that it provokes emotional and physical illness. It is unfortunate, therefore, that the association between conscience and peace of mind is not analyzed and discussed more freely. Such attention could alleviate conflicts involved in personal and family life.

This may be one of the most relevant questions we can ask of ourselves and of others. Related questions are: Why am I angry? Why am I depressed? Why do I feel lonely? These feelings suggest one's conscience is not functioning normally, leading to disturbance of peace of mind. These disturbances cannot be understood without evaluating the role of conscience. What is our level of arousal? Are we heeding its messages. Are we intentionally avoiding them, only to have them occur over and over again so that peace of mind is far away?

Peace of mind, perhaps the greatest of all gifts, has been sought for centuries. A certain level of tranquility is essential for health and sanity. However, this need is not considered in relation to conscience. It is time we do. Perhaps, no other factor is of greater significance insofar as peace of mind is concerned. Physical abilities and occupational success are of little influence. Peace of mind is of greater relevance than ever in view of the stress, violence, and upheaval present in society. Conscience is a critical factor because it involves all levels of life—personal, occupational, and social. The level of peace of mind each of us achieves is the basic indicator of successful living; no other factor comes close to being as important.

Many disturbances come from outside sources, but it is the turmoil within ourselves that is more threatening and debilitating. Tranquility cannot be attained at the expense of conscience. The extent to which one attains a normal conscience determines his level of peace. Warnings from conscience should not be threatening. Kochansky says there are "few developmental issues more central to socialization than the development of conscience" (p. 325). He concludes that impulsivity and poor judgment in adulthood result from an unpredictable, chaotic environment in early childhood. Only when we have developed a moral code on which we can depend can we feel confident, not hampered by anxiety and depression. Our value system gives us impetus to pursue goals with positive feelings, confident that our self-control has the strength we need to meet life's challenges.

The results for this question are remarkable. Scoring highest are the senior citizens, 75% of whom say conscience interferes with peace of mind; more than half of the other Americans also say *yes*. We find these results troublesome. Why do so many people have a conscience that disturbs peace of mind? Why do senior citizens more than any other group find this to be the case? The implication is that we are not understanding the role of conscience, how it is the center of meaning, the guide to joyful living. Even half of the seminarians find their conscience disturbs peace of mind. But this disturbance seems to be primarily an American experience. The response from the Japanese and Mexicans is in the opposite direction. Two-thirds of the Mexicans say conscience does not disturb peace of mind. Although many of the Japanese say conscience makes them feel remorseful only one-third of them say it interferes with peace of mind. The Japanese, guided by affiliation with a group, and the Mexicans, guided by external rules, do not feel an imposition from conscience on peace of mind as do Americans.

Do You Try to Obey Your Conscience

Obedience to authority concerns following those responsible for setting limits and enforcing laws. Questioning authority is important and should not be feared. However, to assume all authority is damaging or unnecessary is dangerous, serving only to disrupt relationships. Conscience assumes the role of authority because it is the system which alerts us to the implications of our conduct. When well developed it does not put unnecessary demands on decision-making. It is well for us to be reminded of Milgram's (1969) study in which he defines and clarifies what he designates as "crimes of obedience." Such crimes help us understand the most horrifying instances of mass murder. In crimes of obedience individuals ignore messages from conscience and blindly follow the dictates of others irrespective of their degradation and cruelty.

In the question, do you try to obey your conscience, we are studying how seriously one takes the information provided by conscience. Character and integrity are involved because we are asking whether the messages are meaningful. Presumably some persons take these messages seriously and others do not. As indicated previously, if directions from conscience are ignored we might expect immorality to be dominant. Only when conscience is emphasized can we expect character to serve as a pattern for behavior.

Except for criminals and Mexicans all groups responded strongly in saying they try to obey their conscience; senior citizens and clergymen scored highest and criminals the lowest. Prisoners are below normal in arousal and when alerted by conscience give less attention to the messages; another finding significant in understanding criminality.

Mexicans again are an exception. Unlike Japanese whose scores are in close agreement with Americans, 82% of Mexicans say *no*, they do not try to obey their conscience. This response is consistent with their perception of conscience; they attain self-control more through externals such as rules given by parents and do not listen to their conscience. More Japanese than any other group say they try to obey their conscience; they respond uniformly, indicating conscience serves a purpose and is to be followed. There is much agreement between the results for the Americans and the Japanese, but wide differences for the Mexicans.

Do Some People Not Have A Conscience

When we think about conscience it is difficult not to be critical of others. Conduct that ignores conscience occurs at all levels of society, in business, medicine, law, education, and elsewhere. Corruption is so common we are beginning to accept it as the norm, which is frightening. When arousal levels are lowered and we no longer are alerted to evil, we face catastrophic circumstances. It is appalling how our moral values and standards have changed. We accept evils that were formerly considered immoral and unacceptable such as overlooking sexual promiscuity. Lowering our arousal level and showing little concern about evil is threatening and allows "violence in the streets" to continue.

However, in the question, do some people not have a conscience, we are referring to more than what Eigen calls an "immoral conscience." We are inquiring as to whether people believe that certain individuals have no conscience. It is clear that individuals vary widely in manifestations of conscience. We are interested in whether people view others as having no internalized value system, which is pertinent to the broader question of what conscience is and how it relates to self-control. Behavioral scientists continue to find it difficult to demonstrate that certain individuals have a conscience because under certain circumstances people who otherwise show they have a conscience conduct themselves in remarkably immoral ways.

If we believe individuals, groups, or races are without a conscience it reflects on our attitudes toward them, even to the extent of viewing them as less human than others. This question also involves beliefs about the nature of conscience and its role in everyday life. The Japanese scored highest with only one-fourth saying some people do not have a conscience. Their feelings of group conformity cause them to rely on the values of others. They have an internalized value system which serves as a model, reflecting a conscience that characterizes a majority of people.

The Mexicans, senior citizens, and prisoners varied considerably from the Japanese. Mexicans believe that a large number of their fellow citizens do not have a conscience, consistent with their belief that internalized values are of less consequence than external controls in self-discipline. Many Americans also believe some individuals do not have a conscience. The extent to which this belief reflects the state of violence and corruption in our society is not clear but it is a factor. It is difficult to believe people are following their conscience when one must be vigilant about violence and security wherever one goes.

Indirectly these results show that we are not successful in the development of self-control. Senior citizens show the greatest concern about these circumstances. Perhaps they have a reason for feeling less secure in everyday life and have a greater fear of violence. This possibility is reflected in various ways. It is less clear why more than half of the criminals believe some people do not have a conscience. However, this belief seems consistent with their saying conscience as a value system is of less consequence in their lives. Throughout, their responses show lower arousal levels than normal and less awareness of right and wrong, so presumably they believe conscience is of less consequence in the lives of others.

Does Conscience Grow and Develop As We Become Older

Conscience is a dynamic system dependent on training. In our questionnaire we included three items pertaining to its growth: whether conscience is only what we are told as children, whether conscience is the same in children as in adults, and whether conscience grows and develops as we grow older. If conscience were a fixed entity it would not be a critical part of child rearing, not a dynamic system of moral standards developed through training, discipline, education, and religion. The question of whether conscience grows concerns the fundamental issue of how we become sensitive to right and wrong. Are arousal levels a fixed entity as the Mexicans believe? Or is sensitivity to evil a dynamic system that continues to grow throughout our lifetime?

Our postulation says conscience is a self-control process gained through discipline, education, and religious instruction. It varies from person to person but contains shared values to make interpersonal relationships possible, recognizing there are wide variations and many beliefs that must be tolerated if society is to function cohesively. One's understanding of conscience is essential to being able to show tolerance. This question about whether conscience grows as we increase in age concerns beliefs about its being a dynamic system, not a fixed entity.

At a level of 88% criminals say conscience grows as we become older. The Americans express the belief that conscience is not fixed but grows and develops. Japanese are less convinced. This reflects their adherence to the belief that internalized values are secondary to values ascribed by group identity.

Almost all Mexicans say conscience is what one is told as a child and that it is the same for children and adults; only 15% say it grows as we become older. We conclude that they are strongly of the view that it is a fixed entity. Americans believe conscience results from training and without training conscience cannot occur. This is in marked contrast with Mexicans who believe it is static, the result of rules given in childhood. Japanese fall in between with half saying it grows as we become older and half saying it does not. Many Japanese believe the value system established by the group is a standard that is not flexible and does not change with increasing age. Other Japanese believe the value system does change as individuals increase in age. These results may reflect cultural changes occurring in Japan with more emphasis on individual autonomy. Whatever the reason, there is wide variation in their belief about the growth of conscience in relation to age. Again we observe variations on the basis of race and culture.

Does Your Conscience Prevent You From Gaining the Pleasures That You Want

Many people have a negative concept of conscience and think of it as an imposition. Negative attitudes about conscience derive from a mild, moderate, or severe conscience disorder. When conscience is characterized by messages that arouse people about engaging in immoral conduct, everything one does is interpreted as being wrong. When conscience functions in this way it is considered "sick" and assistance should be sought. When conscience functions normally we understand it as the basis for self-control, that it does not cause disturbances in behavior.

In the question, does your conscience prevent you from gaining the pleasures you want, we were interested in obtaining information about people who consider it to be punitive. Unfortunately many persons hold this view. When the messages of conscience are mostly about what is wrong it is either too restrictive or the individual is living immorally. That some persons fall into the category of immoral living is obvious and if they have a functional conscience it will send arousal signals. If conscience is characterized by messages that say we should not engage in legitimate pleasures it must be designated as disordered.

Of the Americans less than half say their conscience impeded them from gaining desired pleasures. Three-fourths say it makes them feel remorseful so we should expect many would feel it impeded gaining pleasures. Even more of the Japanese say conscience inhibits gaining desired pleasures, but it is the Mexicans who feel this restriction most keenly; 70% say it is an inhibiting factor. This is of special interest because Mexicans are less influenced by an internalized value system than other groups. It is consistent, however, with the trend to view conscience in a negative way. Their belief seems to be that rules are necessary for conduct although they are inhibiting and disadvantageous.

More Japanese than Americans feel conscience prevents gaining pleasures but they fall below Mexicans. The Americans find conscience to be the least restrictive. This is unusual because both Japanese and Mexicans perceive conscience as less of an internalized value system. For Japanese this may mean group identity is an imposition on gaining pleasures as individuals. For Mexicans, who believe conscience is comprised of rules learned in childhood, it shows that they think rules are inhibiting and prevent them from engaging in pleasurable activities. It appears that conscience as a self-control system is less successful for Japanese and Mexicans. But we cannot overlook the fact that between one-third and one-half of Americans also find that conscience prevents gaining desired pleasures.

A broader involvement of this question concerns the position that pleasure is the main if not the only reason for living, a point of view that is destructive. But pleasures are essential and have a place in our lives. Conscience should not be punitive but it must alert us to obligations and to what it means to be caring, responsible human beings.

Does Your Conscience Interfere
With Maintaining Friendships

Friendships play an important role in our lives. Conscience is fundamental to interpersonal relationships, to forming friendships and being a friend. Interpersonal relationships entail values and friendships more than other relationships involve sharing them. When internalized moral values serve as a guide it is unlikely that friends would be dishonest, cruel, vindictive, or insensitive. A friend is someone for whom we feel a special kindness and tolerance, someone we feel close to, who gives us the feeling of being accepted and needed. Without shared values such feelings are impossible because if conduct is not reciprocal there is conflict. To be friends means that there must be internalized feelings of shared values that go beyond those we share with others. If conflicts arise we face a debate within ourselves which requires us to decide whether to permit others to determine what we do. This decision making is the backbone of virtuous living. It is a vital process ongoing throughout life and determines growth emotionally and spiritually. Conscience cannot be isolated from friendships. In fact, it cannot be isolated from any part of our life. We must have faith in our values and in the way of life we choose, including friendships. Freeman says this conviction is the "centrality of faith" (p. 19). He asks, "can a being that is nothing more than a body transversing space ever bring forth a justifiable reason to be moral rather than immoral, to be good rather than bad, to love rather than hate?" (p. 38). When we choose friends we cannot avoid choosing values. If we choose friends who engage in fraud, violence, and hatred we must take responsibility for the outcome, a message that must be clarified for youth.

Maintaining friendships requires thought, self-discipline, and self-evaluation. If we find that we do not share the values of those close to us we will be in conflict. If we are uncertain of our values, we fear that saying no means we will be rejected. Fear of rejection is a powerful feeling. This is the underlying meaning of the question, does your conscience interfere with maintaining friendships. Many people cannot withstand the feeling of not being accepted and succumb to the values of others even though they may be damaging. In a significant way making friends entails strength of character. To quote Freeman again, "unless we are certain that the ground on which we walk is more or less stable and secure, we will be hesitant to take even the smallest step" (p. 39). We need this confidence when making friends. Society does not clearly reflect the urgency and significance of shared moral values. Kekes warns that "evil is a formidable obstacle to human well-being, and if we care about humanity we must face evil" (p. 3).

Our survey results concerning relationships between conscience and friendship show variations by group. Of Americans, senior citizens and criminals again scored highest with one-third saying conscience interfered with maintaining friendships. More than three-fourths of Mexicans say conscience interferes with friendships. The widest variation appeared for the Japanese, 90% of whom say conscience did *not* interfere with friendships. There is agreement between Mexicans and Americans saying conscience is an imposition on maintaining friends but Japanese are decidedly of the opposite belief. Although Mexicans perceive conscience as being rules imposed externally they find it an imposition on personal relationships. They attribute a high level of influence to conscience as it relates to other people. Japanese do not, relying more on strength of group identity for formation of friendships. Most Americans do not find conscience to be a negative influence on making friends.

Is Conscience Important to Mental Health

Mental health is not given the consideration it warrants. Emotional disorders may be the greatest problem faced by individuals everywhere. When we give attention to the number of people who present problems, have addictions, engage in criminality, and others who have problems in maintaining self-control, we realize that a large segment of the population has emotional disturbances that cause personal and family upheavals, disturbing not only to themselves but to others. That conscience is influential in these dysfunctions cannot be questioned. Again we stress arousal levels. If these levels are highly punitive mental health is jeopardized. If they are too low what is right and wrong cannot be judged adequately. The concept of self-regulation is crucial. Mental health is the outcome of successful self-regulation, and conscience is the system that makes self-discipline possible. Johnson, Dokecki, and Mowrer explain:

> the prevailing supposition on the part of most psychotherapists was that functional personality disorders arise because persons thus afflicted have an excessively severe, rigid, tyrannical conscience; and the remedial efforts commonly involved an attempt to make conscience more flexible, reasonable, permissive. It is now widely recognized that therapy based on this 'diagnosis' has been conspicuously unsuccessful. (p. 38)

A conscience disorder may cause anxiety, remorse, guilt, depression, and other emotional conflicts. Johnson, Dokecki, and Mowrer conclude, "the thrust of the present discussion has been to suggest that in what may be called characterological neurosis, conscience is not the villain, but rather the victim of disregard and mistreatment" (p. 38). Conscience is a basic aspect of mental health but its role has been misunderstood. Our purpose in undertaking this study was to emphasize its role and indicate that it must be properly developed, not eliminated. Our intention is to stress that moral values are the basis for mental health and that these values include the concept of spirituality. Martin and Carlson believe "that there is a growing body of evidence that spiritually oriented life-styles may be associated with reduced incidence of disease and health risk factors, as well as enhanced quality of life" (p. 58).

In answering this question almost all Americans say conscience is important to mental health. The prisoners scored lowest, showing less awareness of the significance of conscience. The Japanese also showed awareness of the significance of conscience in mental health. Mexicans hold what is essentially an opposite belief because almost four-fifths of them say conscience is *not* important to mental health. It appears they perceive mental health as being more related to external factors, not to the internalized values manifested by conscience. They seem unaware of the ways in which conscience and mental health are intertwined. The implication of their belief is not clear but it appears they think of conscience as comprising a set of standards imposed externally and, therefore, of little significance to mental health.

Is Conscience Important to Physical Health

As seen in the burgeoning field of behavioral medicine there is growing awareness of the psychological, moral, and spiritual aspects of health. According to Remen, a pioneer in studying associations between mental and physical health, "the human qualities that we all bring to the experience of disease, qualities such as insight, patience, resourcefulness, ingenuity, wisdom and courage may play as great a role in the recovery of health as the most sophisticated of medical treatment" (p. 7). There is research to support Remen's point of view, but we are not winning the struggle to convince people that their lifestyle and beliefs are crucial in maintaining good health. As shown by diseases such as AIDS and emphysema, behavioral diseases characterize our era. People want and need warmth, friendship, hope, and direction. We do not only wish to prolong life, we want quality too. Unless these inner needs are recognized we face serious consequences, including poor health. Remen emphasizes that caring is a source of energy from which we can gain strength and be of help to others simultaneously. She also says "to formulate meaning is a uniquely human attribute" (p. 197). It is as meaning-makers that we show our greatest human abilities and contribute to health at the deepest level. Meaning and values are directly related so we must ask ourselves whether we are fostering or impeding health, whether we are respecting or denigrating ourselves by the choices we make.

Conscience is the system through which all decisions are made. Stress, one of the common conditions related to health, is a condition through which we are warned that all is not well. Martin and Carlson suggest that "when persons develop strong commitments to their work and its meaningfulness, perceive the tasks that they perform as challenging rather than threatening, and operate with a sense of personal control over their environment, they are less likely to report negative stress or symptoms associated with illness" (p. 65). These investigators report "modern diseases frequently are disorders that stem from living in the fast lane of high stress, addictive over-consumption, fast foods, energy saving devices, and sexual liberation" (p. 75).

Baird studied individuals in poor health and found that those who seek medical assistance often suffer from conscience disorders. He describes these disorders as mainly of two types: those with an excessively harsh conscience and those dealing with guilt feelings in destructive ways. Baird draws an important conclusion when he says that people who are dominated by guilt and self-blaming desire punishment so illness is welcome, serving an emotional need. This conclusion shows conscience disorders must be included in diagnosis and treatment of illnesses. Baird refers to these conditions as "lesions of conscience" (p. 18).

From the point of view of behavioral science, the question is not whether there is an association between emotional disturbances and health, but what the nature of this association might be, the extent of its influence on health, and implications for treatment. Our survey shows almost all Americans, except prisoners, believe conscience is important to physical health. The Japanese also say conscience is important to physical health, in close agreement with Americans. The Mexicans differ with 60% indicating this association is not important.

These results suggest that people are in need of assistance in understanding the role of conscience in their lives. Again the work of Martin and Carlson is helpful. They emphasize that behavioral medicine research is providing information on the importance of belief factors in health and recovery from illness. They stress, "love, marriage and fidelity are the main tenets of most spiritual systems, and violating them causes anxiety, troubled hearts, spiritual and psychological pain, and apparently some major health compromises" (p. 97).

Are the Consciences of Men and Women the Same

It has been assumed that men and women differ in the extent to which they establish and internalize moral values, the assumption being that women have better self-control. However, this belief has not been studied extensively. It is relevant to all aspects of how conscience develops and functions. If gender differences exist they should be studied in relation to how conscience is acquired and why it is better established in one gender in comparison with the other. In a related investigation, Breen and Prociuk studied internal versus external self-control processes and found women were more prone to guilt feelings than men. These results support the opinion that women are superior to men in maintaining self-control.

Our research results are revealing. Senior citizens, clergy, and seminarians believe gender is not a factor in relation to conscience, nor do most Mexicans and Japanese. Criminals fall within the medium range. Our data, group by group, show that conscience function does not vary by gender. If we are negligent in conscience training we are equally so for boys and girls. Efforts to improve training in self-control should apply to both sexes.

Is Conscience Related to Self-Discipline

Although conscience is perceived as the process that sends signals about immoral conduct, its role in self-control is often overlooked. There is substantial agreement among Americans and Japanese showing conscience and self-discipline are related. However, this belief among Americans is held most widely by liberal arts students, clergy, and prisoners. Only a small number of Mexicans believe conscience is a factor in self-discipline. Americans and Japanese believe self-discipline is attained by developing internalized value standards that serve to regulate conduct, that these standards are the basis of self-control. Mexicans are of the opinion that self-discipline is gained through external influences such as rules laid down in childhood.

Is Conscience Important to Your Survival

Behavioral scientists, media commentators, and clergy try to alert us to the seriousness of the chaos, confusion, and violence that surrounds us. Many believe the pattern before us is threatening and that countermeasures are needed. Kekes stresses the role of moral values in everyday life and the need to recognize the power of evil. He says, "the most painful lesson of all is not that our vulnerability to evil is merely a consequence of adverse external causes—we ourselves are also agents of the contingency, indifference and destructiveness that jeopardize the human aspiration to live good lives" (p. 5). The expediency we cherish is nothing but indifference to the degeneration we cause others and ourselves. Expedient people lack commitment and are malevolent. The philosopher Kant maintains "happiness stands in exact relation with morality, that is, with worthiness to be happy" (p. 14). For survival there is need to realize great civilizations have come and gone; stability and progress are possible only to the extent moral values serve as a guide for everything we do.

A large majority of Americans believe conscience is important to survival and that moral values cannot be ignored. Our survey indicates that senior citizens, seminarians, and pastors especially hold this view and to a lesser extent university students and criminals. Most Japanese surveyed agree. The Mexicans hold an opposite view; two-thirds saying conscience and survival are unrelated. Except for Mexicans there is high level awareness of the role conscience plays in survival. Most people recognize that a hedonistic lifestyle of self-indulgence leads to illness and death and that self-control, a system of moral standards, is essential to life and longevity.

Is Conscience Important to Our Survival as a Nation

In our society sensitivity to right and wrong seems to have decreased. We are less concerned about resisting evil so we overlook immoral conduct. How much unconcern can be tolerated without deleterious effects on our way of life is not a frivolous question. We need to think in terms of arousal levels not only as individuals but as a society. The feeling of "community" is basic to a coherent society. We are in the throes of confusion about values. Many do not know what our moral standards are. We need a new awareness of what we believe is right and wrong. This is urgent and should be uppermost in our minds in schools, churches, synagogues, industry, and government. Kilpatrick in his book, *Why Johnny Can't Tell Right From Wrong*, says there is a crisis in moral education; we provide courses in character education without providing a moral foundation for conduct. As a result, he says, we have "created a generation of moral illiterates" (p. 17). He concludes, "if students don't learn self-discipline and respect for others they will continue to exploit each other sexually no matter how many health clinics and condom distribution plans are created" (p. 225).

The results for this question are similar but not identical to those for survival as individuals. Americans and Japanese believe conscience is important to survival as a nation, but as in other responses Japanese fall below Americans. Again, Mexicans essentially hold an opposite belief; three-fourths say conscience and national survival are unrelated. These results are similar to their responses on the relationship between conscience and individual survival. Mexicans are consistent in believing conscience is of little significance insofar as behavior is concerned, personally and as a society. Japanese and Americans, on the other hand, believe conscience is a vital factor.

Are Conscience and Morality the Same

What is right and what is wrong are confusing when morals are viewed as relative, a bewildering situation for youth. The more relativistic we become the more indefinite right and wrong become. Better understanding of conscience would provide a basis for decisions and help us realize the significance of morality. Conscience is an internal, self-evaluation system, and morality is behavior on which society places a value. This does not mean conscience and morality are unrelated. Conscience is the system that makes moral judgments possible and morality is expressed conduct which reflects these values.

Most Americans distinguish between conscience and morality, with more than three-fourths making this distinction. It is revealing that only half of the prisoners believe conscience and morality are not the same. Again we note less sophisticated understanding of conscience and its relationship to conduct. The Japanese were less uniform than Americans. However, the trend for these groups is similar. Mexicans respond with an opposite point of view, eighty-six percent saying conscience and morality are the same. This perception supports their belief that conscience is not an internalized value system but a compilation of external rules and prohibitions.

Have You Asked Yourself Whether You Have
a Well-Developed Conscience

Many people pay little attention to conscience, seeming not to recognize its role. Our survey shows that senior citizens are most aware of conscience, having asked themselves about the status of their conscience. The youngest groups scored lowest. In most groups about half have asked themselves about how well developed their conscience might be; this includes Japanese and Mexicans.

About half of those surveyed think about the extent to which conscience is well-developed. How should these results be interpreted? Should more people show concern about this self-control system? From our point of view it would be advantageous if all people asked themselves about the extent to which their conscience has developed. It is the integration system for establishing standards of right and wrong. This quality of our make-up should be of concern because it is the most important aspect of being a mature human being.

Is the Conscience of People Throughout the World the Same

How we view people in other countries is indicative of how well we relate to them. Are they trustworthy and responsible? These questions arise when we have little information, especially when confronted with those most unlike ourselves. Lack of contact and unfamiliarity leads to labeling on the basis of race and religion or on the basis of how conduct is perceived, as being lazy, treacherous, and dishonest. Labels mean alienation and detachment, not closeness and tolerance. Racism and sexism become outlets for hostility and dehumanization. Many people grow up harboring stereotypes. Only through conscience development can we realize that we are all human beings with certain characteristics and potentials and that everyone needs the humanity of everyone else. Life is a process of change, but conscience is the basis for moral development throughout the world, not only for those whom we include in our immediate circle.

The most remarkable result from our survey is from the Mexicans, the only group believing conscience throughout the world is the same. Their response is highly uniform with 94% giving this response. This is consistent when we recall they believe conscience is a fixed entity comprised of rules laid down in childhood. In comparison only about one-third of Japanese hold this opinion, which is also true of Americans.

The extent to which conscience development differs throughout the world has not been determined. From our results it seems that even in countries that vary greatly in culture there are similarities. Our results show this is the case in Japan and the United States. Also countries close geographically, such as the United States and Mexico, may differ greatly in the way conscience is perceived. Studies of conscience is a way to pursue better understanding of people everywhere.

Have You Talked to Anyone About Your Conscience

Conscience as a self-control system is in need of more consideration, perhaps most urgently in understanding its development. Such consideration is essential in work with children and youth who have a tendency toward being aggressive, abusive, and rebellious. This emphasis might include how conscience serves as the center for moral values, standards of honesty, self-discipline, integrity, and for taking responsibility for oneself. Many youth are curious about growing up and becoming adults, but there are few opportunities for them to engage in discussions about it. Reference to conscience in churches is infrequent, apparently because its importance is not realized.

Mexicans more than any other group say they have talked to someone about their conscience. This was not expected because they perceive conscience as being less significant in conduct. Be that as it may, they seem to have a need to discuss moral issues with others. Conceivably this is because of disagreement about rules comprising their value system.

About half of Japanese say they have talked to someone about their conscience. In comparison most Americans scored lower except for seminarians. Senior citizens and criminals scored lowest with only one-third saying they had discussed their conscience with anyone else.

These results suggest that most people are not inclined to discuss their conscience with others. These results are not surprising. They provide additional evidence for a need to develop programs for definition, discussion, and instruction about the role of conscience in our lives.

CHAPTER VI

A New Awakening

Every human being can be a meaning-maker, a person of vital consequence to ourselves and to those with whom we come in contact. Through conscience we are urged to recognize our unique purpose in life, that we should manifest love, goodness, tolerance, and understanding. Only when conscience is given the thoughtfulness it warrants can life become the highest spiritual adventure imaginable. Through such understanding we gain insights which help us attain our most cherished aspirations. Conscience is a treasured human characteristic which needs consideration far beyond that typically observed.

Children surrounded by anger and rejection of spiritual values cannot internalize feelings of being accepted, cared for, and loved. Instead, feelings of hostility develop and characterize their attitudes, an exceedingly troublesome disability. Children who suffer this tragic situation are at high risk for criminality. No responsible person can overlook what this means. Only when we give attention to this urgency will we reduce juvenile delinquency and adult criminality. Vulnerability to conscience disorders is observable early in life. Our responsibility is to take action to reduce these trends. We need programs for conscience development at all ages, but especially for youth before vulnerability to criminality reaches a peak at 14 years of age. The understanding of what is right and what is wrong is neglected at an unacceptable cost monetarily, but more importantly in terms of human suffering and sacrifice. Violence and aggression are wrong and must be viewed as obsolete. Children and adults must learn to resolve disputes without violence, which means attention must be given to conscience development. Aggression is destructive and not conducive to realizing that others have rights and privileges. In our research we refer to this process as social perception, the ability to perceive our role in relation to those in our immediate environment. There is great urgency for parents and professionals to recognize the meaning of social perception and the disorders that result when conscience is not developed.

Fortunately, many individuals and agencies are prepared to offer help to those in need, but often parents and others are not sympathetic to the needs of children and do nothing, thereby encouraging them to continue on the path to criminality. The destructiveness of the feeling "I am nobody" cannot be exaggerated. Although everyone is someone many children and adults are unable to feel proud of being who they are. One of our greatest challenges is to help the "nobodies" realize they are "somebodies." Every child needs such assurance. Every human being is of immortal value and in need of everyone else. This is the foundation of self-respect and self-respect leads to respect for others.

Our role as meaning-makers is the greatest challenge we have as parents. We must teach the meaning of right and wrong. In teaching children to make this distinction we are helping them develop moral reasoning, our highest level of accomplishment as human beings. This aspect of being human is all but astounding. We not only distinguish between right and wrong but we show love, forgiveness, and understanding, which are transmitted to children in everyday activities, including through the way we discipline them. These values are taught by what we do and by what we say. This is what being a meaning-maker means. Values are consistent, right is right and wrong is wrong. Negative attitudes toward these values lead to the decay of moral standards. Destructiveness gets out of hand. Along with moral reasoning we must emphasize the meaning of forgiveness.

As human beings one of our greatest achievements is to be able to forgive, and conscience is a vital force in this process. We may never forget a traumatic experience with a wife, husband, or child but we can be forgiving if our conscience permits us to do so. An experience of deception, for example, may cause us to have an attitude of vindictiveness: "I'll get you for this." But when our conscience reminds us that vindictiveness will not correct the situation we are on the way to deriving a better solution. Usually conscience tells us that anger begets anger and that there is a better way of resolving the transgression; conscience not only says "no," it also alerts us to the higher value of forgiveness. Teaching forgiveness through what we do and say is meaning-making at a high level. There is no better foundation for using discipline than to change negative behavior because we are transmitting values. Unfortunately, discipline is often used only to convey anger. Our inclination is to say, "if you do that again, I'll get you," telling children punitiveness, anger, and violence are the best means for resolving problems. Our purpose should be to convey that if one's conduct is destructive it will not be tolerated and forms of punishment will follow. Anger is not the basis of this process. We can do no better as meaning-makers than to exemplify that moral reasoning is the foundation for resolving conflicts.

Works Cited

Allport, G. (1955). *Becoming*. New Haven: Yale University Press.

Allport, G. (1951). *The Individual and His Religion*. New York: Macmillan.

Antonovsky, A. (1980). *Health, Stress and Coping*. San Francisco: Jossey-Bass.

Aronfreed, J. (1968). *Conduct and Conscience*. New York: Academic Press.

Assagioli, R. (1972). *The Act of Will*. New York: Penguin Books.

Ausobel, D. (1953). Relationships Between Shame and Guilt in the Socializing Process. In C. Kluckhohn and H. Murray, (Eds.) *Personality in Nature, Society and Culture*. New York: Knopf.

Baird, p. (1982). Lesions of Consequence: Intrapsychic Agent of Self-destruction in Medical Patients. *Psychiatric Forum, 11*(2), 18-25.

Baltes, p. and Smith, J. (1990). Toward a Psychology of Wisdom and its Ontogenesis. In R. Sternberg, *Wisdom*. New York: Cambridge University Press.

Baltes, p. and Staudinger, U. (1993). The Search for a Psychology of Wisdom. *Current Directions in Psychological Science, 2*, 4.

Batson, C., Schoenrade, p. , and Ventis, W. (1992). *Religion and the Individual*. New York: Oxford University Press.

Baumeister, R. (1991). *The Meanings of Life*. New York: Guilford Press.

Baumeister, R. (1993). *Self-esteem—The Puzzle of Low Self-regard*. New York: Plenum Press.

Baumeister, R., Heatherton, T. and Tice, D. (1994) *Losing Control*. New York: Academic Press.

Baumrind, D. (1992). Leading an Examined Life: The Moral Dimension of Daily Conduct. In W. Kurtines, M. Azmitia, and J. Gewritz, *The Role of Values in Psychology and Human Development*. New York: John Wiley & Sons.

Black, D. (1993). *The Social Structure of Right and Wrong*. New York: Academic Press.

Blasi, A. (1984). Moral Identity; It's Role in Moral Functioning. In W. Kurtines and J. Gewirtz, *Morality, Moral Behavior, and Moral Development*. New York: John Wiley & Sons.

Blatt, S. and Homan, E. (1992). Parent-child Interaction in the Etiology of Dependent and Self-critical Depression. *Clinical Psychology Review, 12*, 47-91.

Bloom, A. (1987). *The Closing of the American Mind*. New York: Simon & Schuster.

Boorstin, D. (1993). The Fourth Kingdom. *U.S. News and World Report, 115*(16), 81-82.

Bostrom, J. (1975). The Superego and the Good Life. *Journal of Religion and Health, 14*, (4) 284-93.

Breen, L. and Prociuk, T. (1976). Internal-external Locus of Control and Guilt. *Journal of Clinical Psychology, 32* (2), 301-302.

Bretherton, J. and Waters, E. (1985). Growing Points of Attachment. *Monographs of the Society for Research in Child Development, 209*, 1-2.

Butt, S. (1992). Winners and Other Losers. *Aggressive Behavior, 18*,(4), 318-320.

Carver, C. and Scheier, M. (1981). *Attention and Self-regulation: A Control Theory Approach to Human Behavior*. New York: Springer-Verlag.

Cecil, A. (1987). The Unchanging Spirit of Freedom. In W. Taitte (Ed.) *Traditional Moral Values in the Age of Technology*. Dallas: University of Texas.

Chambers, O. (1935). *My Utmost for His Highest*. New York: Dodd, Mead & Co.

Chazan, R. (1979). The Conscience in Theory and Therapy. *Israel Annals of Psychiatry and Related Disciplines, 17*(3), 189-200.

Choue, L., Johnson, R., Bowers, J. and Darvill, T. (1990). Intrinsic and Extrinsic Religiosity as Related to Conscience, Adjustment, and Altruism. *Personality and Individual Differences,11*(4), 379-400.

Colby, A. and Damon, W. (1992). *Some Do Care*. New York: Free Press.

Coles, R. (1986). *The Moral Life of Children*. Boston: Atlantic Monthly Press.

Condon, J. (1990). *With Respect to the Japanese*. Tokyo: Yaham Publications.

Covey, S. (1990). *The Seven Habits of Highly Effective People.* New York: Simon & Schuster.

Damon. W. (1988). *The Moral Child.* New York: Free Press.

Deutch, M. (1993). Educating for a Peaceful World. *American Psychologist, 48* (5), 510-18.

Doi, T. (1986). *The Anatomy of Self.* Tokyo: Kadansha International.

Dummelow, J. (1978). *A Commentary on the Holy Bible.* New York: Macmillan.

Eigen, M. (1991). The Immoral Conscience. *Psychotherapy Patient,* 7(3-4), 33-44.

Erickson, E. (1981). The Galilean Sayings and the Sense of "I". *Yale Review, 70,* 321-42.

Fairlie, H. (1976). *The Deadly Sins Today.* Notre Dame: University of Notre Dame Press.

Freeman, M. (1993). *Rewriting the Self.* New York: Routledge.

Freeman, M. and Robinson, R. (1990). The Development Within. *New Ideas in Psychology, 8*(1), 53-72.

Gaylin, W. (1984). *The Rage Within.* New York: Simon & Schuster.

Granrose, J. (1967). The Implications of Psychological Studies of Conscience to Ethics. *Dissertation Abstracts, 27*(9A).

Hallesby, O. (1933). *Conscience.* Minneapolis: Augsburg Press.

Harris, p. (1989). *Children and Emotion.* New York: Blackwell, Inc.

Hartman, H. (1960). *Psychoanalysis and Moral Values.* New York: International Press.

Hersen, M., and C. Last (Eds.) (1990). *Handbook of Child and Adult Psychopathology.* New York: Pergamon Press.

Hoffman, M. (1971). Father Absence and Conscience Development. *Developmental Psychology, 4*(3), 400-406.

Holliday, S. and Chandler, M. (1986). *Wisdom: Explorations in Adult Competence.* New York: Karger.

Hutschnecker, A. (1981). *Hope, the Dynamics of Self-fulfillment.* New York: G. p. Putnam's Sons.

Izard, C. (1971). *The Face of Emotion.* New York: Appleton Century Croft.

Jacques, E. (1970). *Work, Creativity and Social Justice.* New York: University Press.

James, J. (1991). *Contemporary Psychoanalysis and Religion.* New Haven: Yale University Press.

Johnson, R., Dokecki, p. and Mowrer, O. (1972). *Conscience, Contract and Social Reality.* New York: Holt, Rinehart and Winston.

Jones, J. (1991). *Contemporary Psychoanalysis and Religion.* New Haven: Yale University Press.

Jones, S. (1994). A Constructive Relationship for Religion with the Science and Profession of Psychology. *American Psychologist, 49*(3), 184-199.

Kagan, J. (1984). *The Nature of the Child.* New York: Basic Books.

Kant, I. (1953). *Critique of Pure Reason.* London: Macmillan.

Katz, F. (1993). *Ordinary People and Extraordinary Evil.* Albany: State University Press.

Kegan, R. (1982). *The Evolving Self.* Cambridge: Harvard University Press.

Kekes, J. (1990). *Facing Evil.* Princeton: Princeton University Press.

Kelman, H. and Hamilton, V. (1989). *Crimes of Obedience, Toward a Social Psychology of Authority and Responsibility.* New Haven: Yale University Press.

Kendal, p. (Ed.) (1991). *Child and Adolescent Therapy.* New York: Guilford Press.

Kilby, R. (1993). *The Study of Human Values.* San Jose: San Jose State University.

Kilpatrick, W. (1992). *Why Johnny Can't Tell Right from Wrong.* New York: Simon & Schuster.

Kitwood, F. (1990). *Concern for Others, A New Psychology of Conscience and Morality.* London: Routledge.

Klinger, E. (1977). *Meaning and Void.* Minneapolis: University of Minnesota Press.

Kochansky, G. (1993). Toward a Synthesis of Parental Socialization and Child Temperament in Early Development of Conscience. *Child Development, 64*(2), 325-347.

Kolenda, K. (1988). *Organizations and Ethical Individualism.* New York: Praeger.

Kroy, M (1974). *The Conscience, A Structural Theory.* New York: Wiley.

Leavy, S. (1988). *In the Image of God.* New Haven: Yale University Press.

LeBlanc, M. (1992). Family Dynamics, Adolescent Delinquency and Adult Criminality. *Psychiatry: Interpersonal and Biological Processes, 55(4)*, 336.

Ledereq, J. (1962). *Christ and the Modern Conscience*. New York: Sheed & Ward.

Lehman, p. (1973). The Decline and Fall of Conscience. In C. Nelson, *Conscience*. New York: Newman Press.

Lewis, H. (1990). *A Question of Values*. St. Louis: Harper & Row.

Loevinger, J. (1976). Origins of Conscience. *Psychological Issues* 9(4, Mono 36), 265-97.

Long, E. (1953). *Conscience and Compromise*. Philadelphia: Westminster Press.

Lytton, H. (1990). Child and Parent Effects in Boys' Conduct Disorders. *Developmental Psychology, 26*(5), 683-697.

Macquarrie, J. (1973). The Struggle of Conscience for Authentic Selfhood. In C. Nelson, *Conscience: Theological and Psychological Perspectives*. New York: Newman Press.

Magid, K. and McKelvey, C. (1987). *High Risk: Children without Conscience*. Golden, CO: M&M Press.

Manchester, W. (1993). The World Lit Only by Change. *U.S. News and World Report, 115*(16), 6-9.

Marcel, G. (1954). *The Decline of Wisdom*. London: Harvill Press.

Martin, J. and Carlson, C. (1988). Spiritual Dimensions of Health Psychology. In W.Miller and J. Martin, *Behavior Therapy and Religion*. London: Sage Publications.

McNeil, J., (1951) *A History of the Cure of Souls*. New York: Harper.

Mead, M. (1953). Social Change and Cultural Surrogates. In C. Kluckhohn and H. Murray,(Eds.) *Personality in Nature, Society, and Culture*. New York: Knopf.

Meninger, K. (1973). *Whatever Became of Sin*. New York: Hawthorn Books.

Merton, T. (1979). *Love and Living*. New York: Harcourt Brace.

Messner, E. (1982). How Elective Public Office Allays Conscience. *American Journal of Orthopsychiatry, 52*, 549-552.

Meyers, D. (1992). *The Pursuit of Happiness*. New York: William Morrow & Co.

Milgram, S. (1974). *The Individual in a Social World*. New York: Reading, Addison-Wesley.

Milgram, S. (1969). *Obedience to Authority.* New York: Harper Row.

Mixon, D. (1989). *Obedience and Civilization.* London: Plato Press.

Myklebust, H. (1994). *Understanding Ourselves as Adults.* Lake Worth: Gardner Press.

Narramore, S. (1974). Where Psychology and Theology Meet. *Journal of Psychology and Theology, 2*(1), 18-25.

Nathanson, D. (1987). *The Many Faces of Shame.* New York: Guilford Press.

Nelson, C. (1973). *Conscience.* New York: Newman Press.

Nelson, C. (1978). *Don't Let Your Conscience be Your Guide.* New York: Paulist Press.

Nelson, T. (1993). The Hierarchical Organization of Behavior: A Useful Feedback Model of Self-regulation. *Current Directions in Psychological Science, 2*(4), 121-26.

Nelson-Jones, R. (1987). *Personal Responsibility Counseling and Therapy.* New York: Hemisphere Publishing Co.

Nichols, M. (1991). *No Place to Hide.* New York: Simon & Schuster.

Nickerson, R. (1992). *Looking Ahead.* Hillsdale: Lawrence Erlbaum.

Peck, M. (1983). *People of the Lie.* New York: Simon & Schuster.

Peele, S. and Brodsky, A. (1991). *The Truth About Addiction and Recovery.* New York: Simon & Schuster.

Raine, A. (1993). *The Psychopathology of Crime.* San Diego: Academic Press.

Rehwinkel, A. (1956). *The Voice of Conscience.* St. Louis: Concordia Publishing House.

Remen, N. (1980). *The Human Patient.* Garden City: Anchor Press/Doubleday.

Reynolds, W. (Ed.) (1992). *Internalizing Disorders in Children and Adolescents.* New York: Wiley.

Roberts, C. (1967). *The Scientific Conscience.* New York: George Braziller.

Roof, W. (1993). *A Generation of Seekers.* San Francisco: Harper.

Salovey, p. (1991). *The Psychology of Jealousy and Envy.* New York: Guilford Press.

Sandin, R. (1992). *The Rehabilitation of Virtue.* New York: Praeger.

Scharzer, R. (1992). *Self-efficacy: Thought Control of Action.* Washington: Hemisphere Publishing Corporation.

Scheier, M. and Carver, C. (1988). A Model of Behavioral Self-regulation: Translating Attention into Action. In L. Berkowitz (Ed.) *Advances in Experimental Social Psychology, Vol. 21.* New York: Academic Press.

Schulman, M., and Mekler, E. (1985). *Bringing up a Moral Child.* Reading: Addison Wesley.

Smith, L. (1980). Science and Conscience. *American Scientist, 68,* (5), 554-58.

Snyder, C. (1994). *The Psychology of Hope.* New York: Free Press.

Solnit, A. (1972). Youth and the Campus: The Search for a Social Conscience. *Psychoanalytic Study of the Child, 27,* 98-105.

Sperry, R. (1993). The Impact and Promise of the Cognitive Revolution. *American Psychologist, 48*(8), 878-85.

Steele, C. (1988). The Psychology of Self-affirmation. Sustaining the Integrity of the Self. In S. Berkowitz, *Advances in Experimental Social Psychology, Vol. 21.* New York: Academic Press Inc.

Sternberg, R. (1990). *Wisdom: Its Nature, Origins, and Development .* New York: Cambridge University Press.

Stilwell, B., Galvin, M., and Kopta, S. (1991). Conceptualization of Conscience in Normal Children and Adolescents. *Journal of the American Academy of Child and Adolescent Psychiatry, 30*(1), 16-21.

Straus, M. (1994). *Beating the Devil out of Them.* New York: Lexington Books.

Taggart, S. (1994). *Living as If.* San Francisco: Jossey-Bass.

Taylor, G. (1981). Integrity. *Proceedings of the Aristotelian Society, LV,* 144-59.

Tesser, A. (1988). Toward a Self-evaluation Maintenance Model of Social Behavior. In L. Berkowitz (Ed.) *Advances in Experimental Social Psychology, Vol. 21.* New York: Academic Press.

Thoreson, C. and Mahoney, M. (1974). *Behavioral Self-control.* New York: Holt, Rinehart and Winston.

Toch, H. (1992). *Violent Men—An Inquiry into the Psychology of Violence.* Washington, D.C.: American Psychological Association.

Toffler, A. (1970). *Future Shock.* New York: Random House.

Wallach, A. and Wallach, L.(1983). *Psychology's Sanction for Selfishness*. San Francisco: W.H. Freeman.

Wallach, A and Wallach, L. (1990). *Rethinking Goodness*. Albany: State University Press.

White, G. and Mullen, p. (1989). *Jealousy*. New York: The Guilford Press.

Wiggins, D. (1987). Needs, Values, Truth. *Aristotelian Society Series, No. 6*. Oxford: Basil Blackwell.

Williams, D. (1989). Experience and Appearance in America's Moral Wilderness. *The Cresset*, 52, 4.

Williams, R. (1968). The Concept of Values. In E. Sills (Ed.), *International Encyclopedia of the Social Sciences, Vol. 16*. New York: Macmillan and the Free Press.

Wolf, S. (1994). The Power Within. *Hemispheres*. United Airlines, February, 15.

Wurmser, L. (1987). The Veiled Companion of Narcissism. In D. Nathanson, *The Many Faces of Shame*. New York: Guilford Press.

The Conscience Questionnaire

(Numbers represent percent answering yes)

QUESTION	A	B	C	D	E	F	G	H
1. Were you born with a conscience?	53.9	64.4	61.1	70.3	90.3	52.9	66.7	69
2. Is conscience a universal human characteristic?	79.5	82.9	92.1	86.6	84.8	0	94.1	78.6
3. Does conscience represent only what you were told as a child?	7.4	12.6	0	2.3	17.9	98.1	43.1	12.7
4. Does your conscience represent only what you believe to be right or wrong?	95.6	96.2	97.3	91.3	96.2	23.1	56.9	90.5
5. Is conscience related to religious beliefs?	87.7	85.6	97.4	89.8	79.8	40.0	37.3	54.8
6. Is the conscience of children the same as that of adults?	5.4	9.6	5.3	16.4	21.6	98.1	19.6	15.1
7. Do you listen to your conscience?	97.3	95.2	97.4	100	98	7.8	90.2	85.7
8. Does your conscience help you?	98	95.2	100	99.2	100	7.8	90.2	85.7
9. Does your conscience cause you to feel shameful?	82	86.7	71.1	81.3	85.8	50	58.8	66.7
10. Does your conscience represent your values?	93.2	94.3	97.4	91.5	95.1	17.3	76.5	81
11. Do you bribe your conscience?	51.5	50.5	52.6	53.2	35	66.7	68.6	35.7
12. Are you afraid of your conscience?	34.1	32.4	13.2	19	36.9	86.5	25.5	31.7
13. Does your conscience interfere with feelings of self-esteem?	56.4	56.2	47.4	50	69.7	51.9	29.4	47.6
14. Does your conscience cause you to feel anxious?	72.4	70.9	71.1	68.8	82.2	62.7	35.3	67.5
15. Does your conscience cause you to feel depressed?	56.9	61.2	31.6	53.1	61.5	66	27.5	57.9
16. Does your conscience cause you to feel remorse?	71.6	73.1	78.9	81.3	73	31.4	78.4	77
17. Is it possible to follow your conscience in everyday life?	70.6	67.6	92.1	78	72.1	68	86.3	73.8

18. Does your conscience interfere with peace of mind?	64.7	58.7	50	61.5	75.7	33.3	31.4	54.8
19. Do you obey your conscience?	93.2	94.1	92.1	97.6	98.1	17.3	94.1	82.5
20. Do some people not have a conscience?	42	46.6	34.2	35.4	63	75.5	23.5	50
21. Does conscience grow and develop as we become older?	95.3	93.1	92.1	93	88.5	15.4	51	88.1
22. Does your conscience prevent you from gaining the pleasures that you want?	41.8	42.2	36.8	37.2	43.3	70.6	45.1	36.5
23. Does your conscience interfere with maintaining friendships?	26.5	21.6	26.3	30	37.4	76.9	5.9	38.9
24. Is conscience important to mental health?	96.3	93.2	100	100	98.1	17.3	88.2	84.9
25. Is conscience important to physical health?	88.5	76.9	94.7	93.8	98.1	41.2	76.5	81
26. Are the consciences of men and women the same?	21.1	25.5	55.3	40.5	45.3	58.8	49	38.9
27. Is conscience related to self-discipline?	93.9	91.3	86.8	86.7	97.1	25	82.4	81
28. Is conscience important to your survival?	84.7	80.8	91.9	90.7	92.2	32.7	76	81.7
29. Is conscience important to our survival as a nation?	92.9	83.7	97.4	93.8	93.2	17.3	74.5	85.7
30. Are conscience and morality the same?	25.9	34.3	24.3	18.6	46.6	86.3	47.1	34.9
31. Have you asked yourself whether you have a well-developed conscience?	36.4	32.7	52.6	46.2	62.9	59.6	47.1	43.7
32. Is the conscience of people throughout the world the same?	7.7	9.6	13.2	11.7	19.4	94.2	37.3	16.7
33. Have you talked to anyone about your conscience?	40.2	38.1	71.1	48.1	36.2	59.6	47.1	34.9

A - Liberal Arts college students   E - Senior Citizens
B - State institution college students   F - Mexicans
C - Seminary students   G - Japanese
D - Lutheran pastors   H - Prisoners